INDEX.

CHAPTER I.

Rules for the Household................................... 1

CHAPTER II.

Beverages...... 6

CHAPTER III.

Bread.. 15

CHAPTER VIII.

CHAPTER IX.

CHAPTER X.

CHAPTER XXII.

COURSE OF INSTRUCTION

AS GIVEN BY

"The Settlement" Cooking Classes.

"THE SETTLEMENT"
COOK BOOK

"The Settlement" Cook Book.

CHAPTER I.

RULES FOR HOUSEHOLD.

FOOD.

Food is anything that nourishes the body. Food is classified thus:

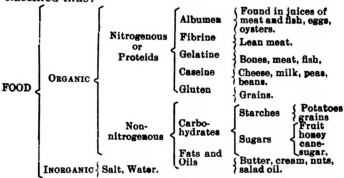

Average adult requires daily: 3½ oz. proteid, 10 oz. starch, 3 oz. fat, 1 oz. salt, 5 pints water.

Relative Value of Foods—It has often been claimed that an egg was equal to a pound of beef in nutrition. Such is not the case, though eggs stand high on the list. The following comparison will no doubt be inter-esting:

	Water, etc.	Muscle Making.	Heat and Fat Making.
Beef	50.0	15.0	30.0
Turkey	44.7	22.9	16.1
Eggs in shell	79.0	15.0	27.0
Oysters (solid)	78.2	12.8	1.6
Milk	86.0	5.0	8.0
Butter	....	....	all
Cheese	10.0	65.0	19.0
Potatoes	75.2	1.4	22.5
Oatmeal	13.6	17.0	66.4
Wheat Bread	14.0	14.6	69.4

MEASURING.

A half-pint cup is the standard. They can be had with fourths and thirds indicated.

A cupful is a cup filled LEVEL with the top.

A spoonful is a spoon filled LEVEL with the top. Run the back of a case knife along the bowl of spoon, to level off the top.

Half a spoonful is obtained by dividing through the middle lengthwise.

A speck of anything is what will lie within a space ¼ inch square.

3 teaspoons equal 1 tablespoon.
4 tablespoons equal ¼ cup.
2 cups granulated sugar equal 1 pound.
2 cups butter equal 1 pound.
4 cups sifted flour equal 1 pound.
2 cups solid meat equal 1 pound.
2 tablespoons butter, sugar, salt, equal 1 ounce.
1 tablespoon liquid equals ½ ounce.

SETTING THE TABLE.

If possible, have a table with square ends. Use clean linen, no matter how coarse and cheap. Have the cloth long and wide enough to hang well around the table. Under the linen cloth have another cloth of some other soft and heavy material. Place the center of the table-cloth in the center of the table, smooth it into place, and have the folds straight with the edge of the table.

RULES FOR PLACING THE DISHES.

The table should look as neat and attractive as possible. Place everything straight upon the table. Turn no dishes upside down. A waiter passes food to the left side of each person, except beverages, which should be placed at the right. In placing a dish in front of a person, the waiter should stand at the right. Food and dishes are removed from the right. To clear the table, remove all dishes from each place, then the meat and vegetables. Remove crumbs from the cloth before bringing in dessert.

RULES FOR WAITING ON THE TABLE.

Always heat the dishes in which warm food is served. Never fill the glasses and cups more than three-quarters full. When passing a plate, hold it so that the thumb will not rest on the upper surface. When refilling the glasses, take hold of them near the bottom and draw them to the edge of the table, then remove them from the table. In passing dishes from which a person is to help himself to a portion, pass it always from the left side, so that it may be taken with the right hand. Place the dish on a tray and hold it low and near to the person who is being served. In passing individual dishes from which the person does not help himself— such as coffee, etc.—set it down slowly and easily from the right hand side. When the dishes are being served by a person at the table, stand at the left hand of that person, hold your tray low and near the table, and take on the tray one plate at a time and place it before the person for whom it is intended, setting it down from the right side. Serve first the most honored guest. When one course is finished, take the tray in the left hand, and stand on the left side of the person you are waiting upon, and remove with your right hand the spoons, knives and forks. Then remove the plate and small dishes, never piling them on top of each other, but removing them one at a time. Fill the glasses before every course. Before the dessert is served, remove the crumbs from the cloth, either with a brush or crumb knife. Do not let the table become disordered during the meal. The hostess should serve the soup, salad, dessert and coffee, and, at a family dinner, the vegetables and entrées. The host serves the fish and meat.

TO CLEAR THE TABLE AFTER A MEAL.

Brush the crumbs from the floor. Arrange the chairs in their places. Collect and remove the knives, forks and spoons. Empty the cups and remove them. Scrape off the dishes—never set any food away on the dishes used for serving—pile them up neatly and remove to the place where they are to be washed. Brush the crumbs from the cloth and fold it carefully in the old crease, as it lays on the table. If the napkins are used again, place them neatly folded in their individual rings.

WASHING DISHES.

Have a pan half filled with hot water. If dishes are very dirty or greasy, add a little washing soda or ammonia.

Wash glasses first. Slip them in sideways, one at a time, and wipe instantly.

Wash the silver and wipe at once, and it will keep bright.

Then wash the china, beginning with the cups, saucers, pitchers, and least greasy dishes, and changing the water as soon as cool or greasy.

Rinse the dishes in a pan of scalding water, take out and drain quickly.

Wipe immediately.

Then wash the kitchen dishes, pots, kettles, pans, etc.

A Dover egg-beater should not be left to soak in water, or it will be hard to run. Keep the handles clean, wipe the wire with a damp cloth immediately after using.

Kitchen knives and forks should never be placed in dish water. Scour them with brick dust, wash with dish cloth, and wipe them dry.

Tinware, granite ironware should be washed in hot soda water, and if browned, rub with sapolio, salt or baking soda. Use wire dish cloth if food sticks to dishes.

Keep strainer in sink and pour all dish water, etc., in it, and remove contents of strainer in garbage pail.

Wash towels with plenty of soap, and rinse thoroughly every time they are used.

Hang towels up evenly to dry. Wash dish cloths.

Scrub desk boards with brush and sapolio, working with the grain of the wood, rinse and dry.

When scrubbing, wet brush and apply sapolio or soap with upward strokes.

Wash dish pans, wipe and dry.

Wash your hands with white (castile or ivory) soap, if you wish to keep smooth hands, and wipe them dry.

Wash teakettle.

Polish faucets.

Scrub sink with clean hot suds.

TO BUILD A FIRE.

It is necessary to have:

1st, Fuel.—Something to burn.

2nd, Heat.—To make fuel hot enough to burn.

3rd, Air.—To keep the fire burning.

TO DUST A ROOM.

Begin at one corner and take each article in turn as you come to it. Dust it from the highest things to the lowest, taking up the dust in the cloth. Shake the duster occasionally in a suitable place, and when through, wash and hang it up to dry.

In sweeping a room, sweep from you, holding the broom close to the floor.

CHAPTER II.

BEVERAGES.

GENERAL RULES.

A beverage is any drink. Water is a beverage, and is an essential to life. All beverages contain a large percentage of water, and aid to quench thirst, to introduce water into the system and regulate the temperature; to assist in carrying off waste; to nourish; to stimulate the nervous system and various organs. Freshly boiled water should be used for making hot beverages; freshly drawn water for making cold beverages.

MILK.

COMPOSITION OF MILK.

Proteids, 3.4%.	Lactose, 4.9%.
Mineral matter, 7%.	Fat, 4%.
	Water, 87%.

GENERAL RULES.

Vessels used for milk must be thoroughly cleansed; they should be first washed in clear, cold water. Fill them with water in which a teaspoon of borax or bicarbonate of soda has been dissolved, and let stand one hour. Then scald, wipe thoroughly, and stand in the sun or near the stove to dry.

Cover milk with muslin and keep in a cold place. Milk may be sterilized or pasteurized to destroy disease germs.

In summer, milk should be sterilized twice a day, for babies or young children.

STERILIZED MILK.

Sterilize milk bottles or jars by boiling them twenty minutes in water. Remove them, fill two-thirds full of milk, and cork with baked or absorbent cotton, or with rubber corks which have been sterilized. Place the bottle on a wire stand in a kettle of hot water, heat the water gradually, until a scum forms over the top of the milk. Keep it at that temperature forty minutes; then remove the bottles and cool them quickly by placing them in cold or iced water. Keep the bottles in a cool place.

FILTERED COFFEE.

1 cup coffee, finely ground,   6 cups freshly boiling
water.

Place coffee in strainer, strainer in coffee pot and pot over slow fire. Add gradually the boiling water and allow it to filter or drip. Cover between additions of water. If desired stronger, refilter. Serve at once, with cut sugar, cream or scalded milk. Put sugar and cream in cup, then add the hot coffee.

BOILED COFFEE.

1 heaping teaspoon ground   1 cup ground coffee to
coffee to   1 qt, freshly boiling water.
1 cup of freshly boiling
water,

Mix the coffee with a clean eggshell and a little cold water, and place in a well aired coffee pot. Add the freshly boiling water, and boil five minutes. Let stand on back of stove ten minutes, Add one-half cup cold water.

NOTE—Coffee should be freshly ground and kept in air-tight cans. A favorite coffee is 2-3 Java and 1-3 Mocha.

CHOCOLATE.

1 qt. milk, or   ⅓ cup sugar,
1 qt. milk and water   2 oz. chocolate.
mixed,

NOTE—One ounce chocolate equals one small square.

Melt the chocolate over hot water, or in the oven, add the sugar, and then the hot liquid slowly. Boil five minutes directly over the heat; beat well and serve. If the sweet chocolate is used, omit the sugar.

COCOA.

1 cup milk,	2 teaspoons cocoa,
1 cup cold water,	2 scant teaspoons sugar.

Scald the milk. In a sauce pan put the cocoa, sugar and cold water. Boil one minute, then add it to the scalded milk. Taste, and add more sugar, if needed.

TEA.

1 teaspoon tea,	1 cup freshly boiling water.

Pour the water on the tea in an earthen teapot. Let stand five minutes, strain and serve.

FLAXSEED TEA.

1 tablespoon flaxseed,	Juice of 1 lemon,
1 tablespoon sugar,	1 cup cold water.

Wash the flaxseed thoroughly, put it with the cold water into a sauce pan. Let it simmer one or two hours. Add lemon juice and sugar to taste. Serve hot.

COLD DRINKS.

ICED TEA.

Strain freshly made tea into glasses one-third full of cracked ice. Sweeten to taste. A slice of lemon may be added, seeds removed.

LEMONADE.

1 lemon.	2 cups water.
4 tablespoons sugar,	

Extract the juice of one lemon with a lemon squeezer. Add the sugar and water and stir till dissolved. Add chipped ice if desired.

NOTE—The water may be poured over the sugar boiling hot, in which case, cover and allow to stand until cool, and then add the lemon juice.

ORANGEADE.

Follow same rule as for lemonade, adding a little lemon juice.

LEMONADE FOR 150 PEOPLE.

5 doz. lemons, squeeezd,	6 pounds sugar,
1 doz. oranges, sliced,	6 gallons water,
1 can or a fresh pineapple,	Ice.

The rule is one pound of sugar to every dozen of fruit. If pineapple is fresh, add one more pound of sugar. Mix sugar with fruit and juice, and let stand. When ready to serve add water and ice, to keep cool.

NOTE—The sugar and some water may be boiled to a syrup, allowed to cool, and the fruit and juices added afterward.

LEMON WHEY.

1 cup hot milk,	2 teaspoons sugar,
	1 small lemon.

Heat the milk in a double boiler, add the juice of the lemon. Cook until the curd separates, then strain through a cheese cloth. Add the sugar. Serve hot or cold.

RHUBARB WATER.

Wash the rhubarb, cut in one-half inch lengths. Put into a bowl, add the peel, sugar and boiling water. Cover and set away to cool. Strain and serve cold. Pink stalks will give the water a pretty color.

GRAPE CORDIAL.

¼ cup grape juice,   ¾ cup cold water,
1 teaspoon lemon juice,   Sugar to taste.

Mix sugar with strained grape juice, add lemon juice and water. A slice of orange or pineapple may also be added.

ALBUMENIZED MILK.

½ cup milk,   White of 1 egg.

Put white of egg in a tumbler, add milk, cover tightly, and shake thoroughly until well mixed.

EGG NOG.

Beat the yolk of one egg, add one tablespoon sugar, and beat until light. Add one-half cup of milk. Beat the white of the egg well and fold it in lightly. Add one-half teaspoon vanilla or a little grated nutmeg.

MANHATTAN COCKTAIL.

⅓ whiskey (Sheridan rye),   ⅓ Vermuth bitters,
                           ⅓ water.

And add a dash of angostura, apricotine and orange bitters, and a slice of lemon peel. Sweeten to taste.

WASHINGTON PUNCH FOR 12 PEOPLE.

One-half pineapple, sliced fine and sprinkle liberally with granulated sugar. Add one-half bottle Rhine or Moselle wine, and set aside for twenty-four hours to ripen; then strain and add two bottles Rhine wine, one bottle claret, and the remainder of the pineapple, sliced fine. Just before serving, add one quart champagne. Either use a large piece of ice to cool, or have the wines ice cold before mixing.

EGG MILK PUNCH.

One egg, three teaspoons fine sugar, fill half full ice, one wineglass brandy, two tablespoons St. Croix rum, fill with milk, shake well and strain into large glass, grating nutmeg on top.

CHAMPAGNE PUNCH FOR 12 PEOPLE.

3 qts. champagne,	¼ lb. loaf sugar,
¼ pt. maraschino,	2 lemons, sliced fine,
½ pt. imported brandy,	2 oranges, sliced fine,

Or any fruit in season. If not sweet enough, add more sugar. Just before using, add a large piece ot ice.

CLARET CUP No. 1.

3 lemons (juice),	3 pts. claret,
6 tablespoons sugar,	1 pt. apollinaris,
1 sherry glass curacoa,	1 finely sliced orange.
1 slice cucumber rind, and a bunch of fresh mint,	strawberries, pineapple.

CLARET CUP No. 2.

1 pt. claret,	Juice of 1 orange,
1 cup sugar,	1 slice cucumber rind,
1 pt. sparkling Moselle,	1 pt. apollinaris.

POUSSE CAFE.

⅔ crème de café,	⅙ apricotine or van-
⅙ crème de menthe,	illa.

Pour the café first and slowly add apricotine or vanilla and then the mint.

ORANGE JULEP.

Peel very thin one-half fine orange rind, put it into a glass with a little finely chopped ice, two teaspoonfuls of powdered sugar. Stir two minutes to extract the oil. Fill the glass with chopped ice, two sprigs of fresh mint, one small teaspoon of crème de menthe, four tablespoonfuls good whiskey—Sheridan rye is the best.

MINT JULEP.

Large Thin Julep Glass—Dissolve one teaspoon fine sugar in water, one dash Maraschino, one glass whiskey or brandy, as preferred, four or five sprigs mint held to side of glass, leaves up. Fill up with fine ice and do not bruise the mint. Trim with fruits. If preferred mint can be bruised, but above is the regular Southern julep.

FRUIT SYRUPS.

Fruit syrups may be bottled and kept on hand when needed. They are made by boiling sugar and water to a syrup, then adding the fresh fruit juice; cooled and diluted with cold water, when served.

BOTTLE WAX.

Equal parts of beeswax and resin. Melt them together, and dip the corked bottles into the hot mixture until the corks are covered.

LEMON SYRUP.

1 cup sugar,   ⅛ cup lemon juice,
    1 pint water.

Boil sugar and water to a syrup twelve minutes without stirring after sugar is dissolved; add fruit juice; cool, and dilute with water to taste when serving. Lemon syrup may be bottled.

UNFERMENTED GRAPE JUICE.

10 pounds of Concord   3 pounds sugar,
    grapes,   1 cup water.

Heat grapes and water in kettle until stones and pulp separate. Strain through jelly bag; add sugar, heat to the boiling point and bottle. This will make one gallon of juice. Seal the bottles. When served, dilute one-half with water.

Or steam to the boiling point the raw pressed and strained grape juice in bottles and seal.

GRAPE JUICE CORDIAL.

Use Concord grapes. Wash the grapes and pick from stems. Cover with water and put them up to boil, stirring from time to time until the seeds are free. Pour into a cheese cloth bag, and press out the juice. To each quart of juice, add one pound of sugar; heat again, and when at the boiling point, pour into hot bottles, cork, and seal. More or less sugar may be used.

BLACKBERRY CORDIAL.

One case blackberries, add a little water and heat thoroughly, then strain through cheese cloth. To every quart of juice add one pound sugar, and whole cloves and cinnamon (in a small bag). Boil until it thickens, remove from fire and cool, and add whiskey or brandy, one cup to a quart of syrup. Bottle and seal.

GRAPE WINE.

Mash the grapes well and then strain through a cloth. Put the skins, after squeezing them, with barely enough water to cover them. Strain the juice thus obtained into the first portion. Put three pounds of sugar to one gallon of the liquid. Let it stand in a crock or tub, covered with a cloth from three to seven days. Skin off what rises every morning, without disturbing the contents. Put the juice in a cask, leave it open for twenty-four hours; then bung it up and put clay over the bung to keep the air out. Let your wine remain in the cask until March, when it should be drawn off and bottled. Or, if you have no cask pour wine in jugs, allowing the corks to remain very loose; when through fermenting, fill into bottles. After all signs of fermentation cease, put in the corks very tight, and tie or wire them in and seal. Keep in a cool place.

Currant, Blackberry, Elderberry or Rhubarb wines are made the same way, using less sugar for Blackberry and Elderberry wines.

DANDELION WINE.

1 gal. dandelion flowers,	3 oranges, cut in small squares,
1 gal. boiling water,	3 lemons, cut in small squares,
3 lbs. sugar,	1 oz. yeast.

Pick dandelion flowers, early in the morning, taking care not to have a particle of the bitter stem attached. Pour the boiling water over the flowers and let stand three days. Strain and add the rest of the ingredients and let stand to ferment three weeks. Strain and bottle.

CHAPTER III.

BREAD.

COMPOSITION OF BREAD.

Proteids, 9%.   Fats, 2%.
Mineral matter, 1%.   Water, 32%.
Carbohydrate, 56%.

GENERAL RULES.

Flour should be kept in a dry atmosphere. It makes better bread if heated just before using. The yeast must be fresh. Scald the milk or water, then cool until lukewarm. The heat of the oven should be increased slightly the first twenty minutes, then kept even for twenty minutes, and the last twenty minutes it should decrease. Bread should be kept in a clean tin box, and not exposed to moisture.

Yeast is a plant, the small, invisible germs of which are floating in the air. They settle in various places, and when they find a warm, moist, sweet, strength-giving or nitrogenous mixture, they begin to grow. Hot water kills the yeast plant; cold water chills it. Lukewarm liquids should be used.

When the yeast plant grows it causes fermentation, which changes some of the starch into sugar, and then some of the sugar into alcohol and carbon-dioxide or carbonic acid gas. This carbon-dioxide gas raises the dough. If it rises too long, it will make the bread sour. Dough is made light in four ways:

1. By the use of yeast.
2. By the use of baking powder.
3. (a) By the use of soda and molasses.
   (b) By the use of soda and sour milk.
4. By beating air into a mixture.

BREAD.

2 cups warm milk or water,	2 teaspoons salt,
1 tablespoon butter,	1 oz. compressed yeast,
	2 teaspoons sugar,
	Flour.

Heat the milk or water, add the butter, salt and sugar. When lukewarm, add the yeast, which has been dissolved in one-half cup of lukewarm water; add the flour gradually. When stiff enough to handle, turn the dough out on a floured board and knead until it blisters and is soft and elastic. Put it back into the bowl, cover, and let rise in a warm place until double its bulk; divide into loaves or shape into biscuits; place in baking pans and let rise again until double its bulk. Bake one hour in a hot oven, twelve seconds by the hand. Biscuits require more heat and less time to bake. Remove from pans and place in draft if you wish a hard crust. If a soft crust is desired, roll bread in a clean cloth.

SMALL LOAF OF BREAD.

¼ cup milk,	¼ teaspoon sugar,
1 teaspoon butter,	½ yeast cake (½ oz.),
¼ teaspoon salt,	Flour to make dough.

Make same as the above bread. The large amount of yeast allows the bread to be made and baked in three hours, hence practical in giving a complete lesson on bread.

BREAD TWIST.

Take bread dough when ready to shape into loaves. Divide into halves, thirds, fourths, etc., according to the number of strands desired for each loaf. Knead slightly, roll into strands evenly and twist into braids. Place into pans (floured) to rise until very light. Brush them over with water, milk, or the yolk of a well beaten egg, and sprinkle the top with poppy seeds. Bake in hot oven forty-five to sixty minutes, and cool in a draft to form a hard crust.

BREAD STICKS.

Take pieces of raised bread dough, roll ⅜ of an inch thick and 6 inches long. Place in floured pan, far apart, brush tops with beaten yolk of egg and sprinkle with poppy seed (if desired). Let raise and bake in a hot oven until brown a crisp.

ROLLS.

Take bread dough when ready to shape into loaves, and make a long, even roll. Cut into small even pieces, and shape with thumb and fingers into round balls. Set close together in a shallow pan, let raise until double the bulk, and bake in a hot oven from ten to twenty minutes. If crusty rolls are desired, set far apart in a shallow pan and bake well, and cool in draft.

RYE BREAD.

Rye bread is made same as wheat bread, using rye in place of the wheat flour. If desired, one-fourth to one-half the quantity of wheat flour may be mixed with the rye. Caraway seeds sprinkled in the dough makes a desirable flavor. Bake longer than the wheat bread. Oven must be hot, and the crust should be hard. Brush loaves with water to make them shine.

SOFT GRAHAM BREAD.

3 cups graham flour,	¼ cup sugar,
1 cup white flour,	2 tablespoons butter,
1 teaspoon salt,	¾ yeast cake,
½ cup molasses, or	¾ cup warm water.

Dissolve the yeast with a little of the lukewarm water, mix the other ingredients in the order given, and add sufficient lukewarm water to make a soft dough. Cover bowl and set in a warm place. When the dough is light beat it and pour it into the bread pans, filling them half full. When light, bake in a moderate oven.

ENTIRE WHEAT BREAD.

2 cups scalded milk,
¼ cup sugar, or
⅓ cup molasses,
1 teaspoon salt,

1 yeast cake, dissolved
in ¼ cup lukewarm
water,
4⅔ cups of coarse entire
wheat flour.

Add sweetening and salt to the milk; cool, and when lukewarm, add the dissolved yeast cake and flour; beat well, cover, and let rise to double its bulk. Beat again and turn into greased bread pans, having pans one-half full. Let rise and bake. Entire wheat bread should not quite double its bulk during last rising. This mixture may be baked in gem pans.

POTATO SPLIT BISCUITS.

2 large potatoes,
(baked and grated),
2 eggs,
1 cup warm milk,
½ cake compressed yeast,

½ cup butter,
1 tablespoonful sugar,
Salt,
1 qt. sifted flour (scant).

Dissolve yeast in the warm milk. Mix and knead while the potato is hot and set to rise. Add more flour if necessary. Roll thin and cut with small biscuit cutter. Lay two biscuits, one on top of the other in a pan and stand in a warm place. Bake about twenty minutes in a moderate oven. Brush over with sugar and water before placing in the oven.

STEAMING BROWN BREAD.

Brown bread may be steamed by letting stand in a steamer over boiling water, or on a trivet, in a kettle of boiling water. The water should rise to about half the height of the mould. In either case, the mixture is to be placed in a greased, tightly closed mould. The best results are secured when the water is gradually raised to the boiling-point. After this point is once reached, it needs to be maintained until the cooking is finished, about three hours. Even longer cooking is of no disadvantage.

BOSTON BROWN BREAD.

1 cup rye meal,	1 teaspoon salt,
1 cup corn meal,	¾ cup molasses,
1 cup graham flour,	1¾ cups sweet milk, or
¾ teaspoon soda,	warm water.

Mix and sift dry ingredients; add milk and molasses, and place in a covered, greased mould and steam two and one-half hours, or steam in small cups one hour. Fill cups two-thirds full.

BROWN BREAD.

1 cup sweet milk,	1 teaspoon soda,
½ cup New Orleans	½ teaspoonful salt,
molasses,	1½ cups graham
2 tablespoons boiling	flour.
water,	

Add the boiling water to the salt and soda, mix with the milk and molasses and stir with the flour to a smooth batter. Place in covered buttered moulds and steam four hours. This will fill two one-pound baking powder tins two-thirds full.

GINGERBREAD No. 1.

½ cup sugar,	1 tablespoon ginger,
3 tablespoons butter,	1 teaspoon cinnamon,
1 egg,	1 teaspoon soda,
1½ cups flour,	½ cup milk or hot water,
⅛ teaspoon salt,	½ cup molasses.

Mix butter and sugar to a soft, creamy paste; add beaten egg. Mix spices, salt and soda with flour, and add a small portion. Add molasses and milk mixed together, and flour alternately. Bake thirty to forty-five minutes.

GINGERBREAD No. 2.

2 eggs,	½ cup of currants,
½ cup of sugar,	1 teaspoon spices,
1 cup of molasses,	1 teaspoon ginger,
1 cup of sour milk or	1 teaspoon of soda, a
cream,	little salt,
2 tablespoons melted	2½ cups flour.
butter or drippings,	

Mix and bake in a moderate oven.

CURRENT BREAD.

2 pints of flour,	2 cups milk,
3 teaspoons baking powder,	1 cup currants,
	1 egg,
¼ teaspoon salt,	1 tablespoon sugar.

SOFT CORN BREAD.

2 cups yellow corn meal,	2 cups milk,
	2 tablespoons butter,
½ teaspoon salt,	2 eggs.
3 teaspoons powder,	

Sift together the corn meal, salt and baking powder. Scald the milk, and add the butter to it. When the butter is melted add the milk to the meal together with the yolks of the eggs. Beat the whites of the eggs to a stiff froth, and fold lightly in, just before putting into the oven. Bake in a deep pan, in a hot oven about half an hour.

TOAST.

Cut stale bread into slices one-fourth inch thick; dry in the oven. Then put on a toaster or fork, move it gently over heat until dry, then allow it to become a light brown by placing it nearer the heat and turning constantly; or, light gas oven, heat five to eight minutes. Place bread in toaster or pan, one inch from gas, in lower or broiling oven. When brown on one side turn and brown on the other. Bread cut into triangles and toasted are called toast points, and are used for garnishing.

CRISPED CRUSTS.

Cut the crusts of bread into strips one-half inch wide, five inches long and one-half inch thick, and toast in oven to a golden brown.

WATER TOAST.

Dip slices of dry toast into boiling, salted water. Quickly remove and butter.

MILK TOAST.

2 cups milk,	4 tablespoons butter,
2 tablespoons flour,	1 tablespoon salt.

Cook the flour in the melted butter. Add salt and gradually stir in the hot milk. After it thickens, pour this sauce over slices of dry or water toast. Serve hot.

CROUTONS.

Cut pieces of stale bread into cubes and brown in the oven or cook in deep fat.

CRISPED CRACKERS.

Spread common crackers thinly with butter, put in pan and bake to a delicate brown. Serve hot with soups.

CHAPTER IV.

KUCHEN.

YEAST CAKE DOUGH.

1 pint scalded milk,	5 cups flour,
½ cup butter,	Yolks of 2 eggs,
½ cup sugar,	½ oz. yeast,
1 teaspoon salt,	Grated nutmeg.

Warm bowl and flour. Crumble the yeast in a cup with a teaspoon of the sugar, and one-half cup lukewarm milk. Set in a warm place to rise. To the rest of the scalded milk add the butter, sugar, salt, nutmeg, and when lukewarm, the beaten yolks of the two eggs. Use flat wooden spoon and stir in the yeast and the rest of the flour. Mix well, until the dough is smooth and elastic. Cover closely and let rise double its bulk. Divide into four equal parts. Take one part for—

COFFEE OR SUGAR KUCHEN.

Flour the board and take one part of the raised dough from above recipe. Roll one-half inch thick and place in well greased oblong shallow pans. Brush melted butter over the top and sprinkle with sugar and a little cinnamon. Let rise until light and bake a golden brown in a hot oven fifteen to twenty minutes. Remove from pan.

NOTE—To freshen kuchen, place in a hot oven few minutes before using; or it may be cut into slices one-half inch thick and dried or toasted in the oven.

SCHNECKEN.

Take one part of the raised kuchen dough. Roll one-half inch thick and spread well with melted butter. Sprinkle generously with scraped maple, brown or granulated sugar and cinnamon, then roll. Cut the roll into equal parts about one inch thick, and place close together endwise, on a well buttered pan, spread with a layer of brown or maple sugar. Let rise until light, and bake ten to twenty minutes in a hot oven, a golden brown. Remove from pan.

KUCHEN TARTS.

Roll a piece of raised kuchen dough one inch thick on a floured board, cut with biscuit cutter, and place close together in a buttered pan. Let rise until very light. Dip fingers in flour and make a cavity in center of each biscuit, and drop in a bit of jelly or preserves. Bake fifteen to twenty minutes in hot oven.

GOOD KUCHEN.

4 cups flour,	1 cup lukewarm milk,
	1 cent's worth yeast.

Of these ingredients make a sponge.
Add:

3 whole eggs,	½ cup melted butter,
½ cup sugar,	Lemon rind,
	Pinch of salt.

Slightly heat all materials before mixing them together. Beat one-half hour. Let rise in a warm place, make into desired forms, let rise and bake.

Roll kuchen dough one-half inch thick on floured board, spread with melted butter, add chopped walnuts and brown sugar. Roll as jelly roll. Place in greased pan, spread melted butter over top, let rise again and bake well until brown.

BERLINER PFANN KUCHEN.

Make a good kuchen dough, roll one-inch thick, cut into rounds with biscuit cutter. Place a piece of jelly or preserves in the center of one-half of them. Brush edges with white of egg and cover with the other half. Press edges neatly. Place on well floured board, let raise very light and fry in deep fat.

FILLED WALNUT KIPFEL.

¾ lb. fresh butter,	5 eggs,
1 lb. flour,	½ cup sugar,
1 cake yeast,	1 lb. walnuts,
1 tablespoon cream,	Juice of 1 lemon.

Add to the beaten yolks the sugar, vanilla and the yeast dissolved into the cream. Add the flour. Roll the butter into the flour piece by piece. Roll the dough quite thin, cut into small squares, place a small portion of filling in each square. Fold into crescent shapes, place in pan and ice with the beaten whites of the eggs. Let rise two or more hours, bake thirty minutes in a moderate oven.

Filling.—One pound chopped walnuts, the juice of one lemon and sugar to taste.

BUNDT KUCHEN No. 1.

1 cake of yeast (1 oz.),	1 cup lukewarm milk,
	3 cups flour.

No. 1—Set the yeast with a cup of the flour and the milk, and let rise in warm place, and then proceed with the following:

½ cup butter,	4 eggs,
1 cup sugar,	Rind of lemon.

No. 2—Beat one-half cup of butter to a cream, add one cup of sugar, four eggs, one at a time, rind of a lemon, a little grated nutmeg. Now mix part 1 and 2, and add the remaining flour. Have pan well greased. Place dough in pan, let rise very light, and bake 45 to 60 minutes in a moderately hot oven.

BUNDT KUCHEN No. 2.

½ lb. butter,	1 cup milk,
1 cup sugar,	1 lb. flour,
8 eggs, beaten sepa-	1 oz. compressed yeast,
rately,	Raisins, seeded.
⅛ tablespoon salt,	

Scald the milk and when lukewarm add the salt and yeast and one cup of the flour, set aside to rise. Grease Bundt form well and flour lightly. Cream, butter and sugar well, add beaten yolks and beat, then the raised mixture and the rest of the flour and lastly the beaten whites. Pour in Bundt form, let rise until very light and bake brown and well in a moderately hot oven, about forty-five minutes.

SAVARIN.

¾ lb. flour,	3 eggs,
1 cup of milk,	1 oz. compressed yeast,
¼ lb. sugar.	Rind of 1 lemon,
6 oz. butter,	2 tablespoons Maraschino.

Stir milk, yeast and some of the flour, and let it raise. Then add the other ingredients, beat well, and let this raise again. Then bake in a slow oven about one hour. Cut and strew a few almonds in the mould (an oval form) before putting in the dough. Make an icing of two tablespoons sugar, one tablespoon water, when boiled add one tablespoon maraschino.

APPLE KUCHEN.

Cover a well greased oblong tin as thin as possible with raised kuchen dough. Core, pare and cut four or five apples in eighths. Lay them in parallel rows on top of the dough and sprinkle with sugar and cinnamon. Beat the yolk of an egg, add three tablespoons cream, and drip around apples. Bake twenty to thirty minutes in hot oven, or until crust is well baked and apples are soft. Peaches or plums may be used in place of the apples.

POPPY SEED FILLING No. 1.
(For Pie or Kuchen.)

1 lb. ground Poppy seed, 3 eggs.

Sugar to taste, raisins, citron and almonds, a little salt and little syrup. Boil this mixture in boiling milk and have it thick enough, about the consistency of mince meat.

POPPY SEED FILLING No. 2.
(For Pie or Kuchen.)

One cup black poppy seed, ground fine, if coffee mill is used, throw away the first bit. Two tablespoons butter, one tablespoon molasses, one-half cup chopped almonds, one tablespoon chopped citron, one-quarter cup seedless raisins, sweeten to taste. Add two tablespoons milk to thin, boil and when cool, add vanilla.

CHEESE FILLING No. 1.

¼ cup of butter (melt and add to cheese),
1 pint cheese (press dry and put through colander),
½ cup sugar.
¼ cup cream,
Lemon rind or vanilla,
3 eggs beaten, separately.

Mix well and bake on Plain Pie Crust No. 2, until a golden brown and well set.

CHEESE FILLING No. 2.
(For Pie or Kuchen.)

½ cup butter (melt and add to cheese),
1 pint cheese (press dry and put through colander),
¾ cup sugar,
1 cup cream, beaten.
Rind of lemon, grated,
4 eggs beaten separately,
¼ cup washed currants,
¼ lb. blanched almonds, cut fine.

Line a pie plate with pastry or kuchen dough, pour in the mixture and bake until a golden brown and well set.

CHEESE FILLING No. 3.
(For Pie or Kuchen.)

3 eggs (beat the whites separately),
1 pint cheese (press dry and put through colander),
¼ cup sugar,
½ cup rich cream (beaten stiff),
2 teaspoons flour.
Grated rind of half a lemon, or vanilla.

Line a pie plate with plain pastry or kuchen dough, pour in the mixture and bake until well set and brown.

BLUEBERRY FILLING.
(For Pie or Kuchen.)

Wash and pick over one quart of blueberries, line pie plate with dough, sprinkle with bread crumbs. Add the berries, sprinkle with sugar, not too much, and cinnamon, lemon juice, and over all the yolk of an egg beaten with three tablespoons cream. If green grapes or currants can be obtained, seed and strew around in place of the lemon juice. Cherries, stoned, may be used in place of the blueberries.

CHAPTER V.

MIXTURES WITH BAKING POWDER.

GENERAL RULES.

Pure baking powder is made by mixing one part of soda to a little more than two parts of cream of tartar, combining it with corn starch or flour, to insure its keeping. Three level teaspoons of baking powder will raise one pint of flour. Cold milk or water should be used with baking powder. Use pastry flour if possible. The flour must be sifted before it is measured; then mix, and sift the dry ingredients. The eggs are usually beaten whole and the milk added to them, and then added to the dry ingredients. The fat may be melted and added last, but is usually worked into the flour with the finger tips, or cut in with a knife. The oven must be hot and the pans greased, before the mixtures are prepared. They should be put in the oven or baked as soon as they are mixed.

BAKING POWDER BISCUITS.

2 cups flour,	2 tablespoons butter,
3 teaspoons baking powder,	¾ to 1 cup milk or water.
½ teaspoon salt,	

Sift the flour, baking powder and salt, rub in the butter and add enough milk to make a soft dough. Toss on floured board and roll gently with a rolling pin three-fourths inch thick. Cut into biscuits and bake on buttered tins in a hot oven from twelve to fifteen minutes.

ROLLED BISCUITS.

2 cups flour,	2 tablespoons sugar,
3 teaspoons baking powder,	½ cup stoned raisins chopped fine,
⅛ teaspoon salt,	2 tablespoons citron,
2 tablespoons butter,	chopped fine,
⅔ cup milk,	⅛ teaspoon cinnamon.

Mix five first ingredients same as baking powder biscuits. Roll to one-fourth inch thickness, brush over with melted butter and sprinkle with the raisins, citron, sugar and cinnamon. Roll like a jelly roll. Cut in pieces three-fourths inch thick. Place in buttered tins endwise and bake ten minutes in a hot oven. Dried currants may be used in place of raisins.

SHORT CAKE.

2 cups flour,	2 teaspoons sugar,
3 teaspoons baking powder,	½ teaspoon salt,
	¼ cup butter,
	¾ cup milk.

Mix the same as baking powder biscuit. Divide dough in two parts. Roll them out, and place one on top of the other, and bake twelve minutes in a hot oven on a buttered tin. Split and spread with butter. Place strawberries, peaches, or any desired fruit between and on top. Sprinkle with sugar and serve with milk or cream.

WHEAT MUFFINS.

2 cups flour,	1 tablespoon butter,
½ teaspoon salt,	1 teaspoon molasses.
3 teaspoons baking powder,	1 egg,
2 tablespoons sugar,	1 cup milk.

Mix dry ingredients and sieve twice, rub in the butter. Separate the egg. Beat the yolk and add it to the milk and molasses. Mix with the dry ingredients and stir until smooth. Fold in the beaten white of egg and pour into hot, well greased muffin tins. Bake fifteen to twenty minutes in hot oven.

NOTE—Graham, rye, cornmeal, or whole wheat muffins are made the same way, by mixing with the wheat flour one-fourth to one-half the quantity of graham, rye, cornmeal or whole wheat flour.

CORNMEAL MUFFINS.

Cream one-fourth a cup of butter. Add one-half cup of sugar, then two eggs, beaten, without separating, until light-colored and thick. Into this stir, alternately, one cup of milk, two cups of sifted flour, and one cup of corn meal, sifted with four level teaspoonsful of baking powder and half a teaspoonful of salt. Beat thoroughly, and bake about twenty minutes in hot, well-buttered gem-pans.

POPOVERS No. 1.

¼ teaspoon salt,	1 cup milk,
1 cup flour,	1 egg.

Sift flour and salt into a bowl. Beat the egg and add the milk to it, and stir gradually into the flour to make a smooth batter. Beat with egg-beater until full of air bubbles. Fill hot greased gem pans two-thirds full of the mixture. Bake in quick oven until brown and popped over.

POPOVERS No. 2.

3 whole eggs, beaten,	1½ cups milk,
1½ cups sifted flour,	A little salt.

Do not stir much after the milk and flour are added to the eggs. Bake in quick oven until brown and popped over.

LEMON PUFFS.

Beat three yolks with one-fourth pound powdered sugar, a little salt and lemon peel. Whip the whites of three eggs to stiff froth and add to above one-half pound flour. Bake in muffin rings as soon as mixed.

CORN CAKE No. 1.

1 cup flour,	4 teaspoons baking
1 cup cornmeal,	powder,
4 tablespoons sugar,	1 cup sweet milk,
1 egg.	2 tablespoons butter,
1 teaspoon salt,	melted.

Mix the dry ingredients by sifting them together. Add the milk, the well beaten eggs and the butter. Beat well and bake in a shallow pan in a hot oven, twenty minutes.

CORN CAKE No. 2.

Sift together two cups of Indian meal, one cup of wheat flour, one and one-fourth teaspoonfuls of soda, half a teaspoonful of salt, and one-fourth a cup of sugar. Beat one egg until light, add half a cup of sour cream and two cups of thick sour milk, and stir into the dry ingredients. Bake in shallow pans, in a hot oven, about half an hour.

GRIDDLE CAKES.

The griddle must be hot and thoroughly greased.

2 cups flour,	1 teaspoon molasses if
3 teaspoons baking pow- der,	desired,
	2 eggs, well beaten,
½ teaspoon salt,	1 pint milk.

Mix dry ingredients and sift. Beat the egg, add to milk and stir the two mixtures to a smooth batter. Pour the cakes on the hot griddle from the end of a large spoon. When the cakes are full of bubbles, turn with a broad knife and brown the other side.

NOTE—To make a variety, add one-third the quantity cornmeal, graham flour, cooked rice, or moistened bread, etc., to the wheat flour.

RICE GRIDDLE CAKES.

2 cups hot boiled rice,	1 teaspoon salt,
2 cups flour,	1 pint of milk,
3 teaspoons baking pow- der,	2 eggs.

Mix the dry ingredients. The beaten yolks are added to the milk. Combine the two mixtures and lastly fold in the beaten whites. Cook as Griddle Cakes.

CORNMEAL AND RICE GRIDDLE CAKES.

½ cup corn meal,	2 teaspoons baking pow- der,
¼ cup flour,	
1 cup boiled rice,	½ teaspoon salt,
	2 eggs,
	1 cup milk.

Mix dry ingredients. The beaten yolks with the milk. Combine the two mixtures, and fold in the whites beaten stiff. Cook same as other Griddle Cakes.

WAFFLES.

Sift one and three-fourths cups flour, three level teaspoonfuls baking powder, and one-half teaspoonful salt. Add gradually one cupful milk with two yolks, beaten until thick. Add one tablespoonful melted butter and two egg-whites beaten to a stiff froth. Fry on hot, well greased waffle iron. Serve with maple syrup.

SUGAR SYRUP.

2 cups sugar, ⅝ cup water.

Use brown or white sugar. Boil until clear. Stir until the sugar is dissolved, but not afterwards. Cool.

CHAPTER VI.

FRIED CAKES.

GENERAL RULES FOR COOKING IN DEEP FAT.

The fat used for cooking may be vegetable oil, olive oil, rendered butter, beef drippings, goose or duck fat, or a mixture of several fats. Use a deep iron kettle, and have the fat deep enough to float the articles to be cooked. The fat is hot enough for cooking raw foods or batters when a small square piece of bread browns in it while you count sixty. In frying cooked foods (croquettes, fish balls, etc.), the bread must brown while you count forty. Remove the articles fried with wire spoon, on unglazed brown paper. The fat should then be clarified. Allow it to cool, then add a few one-fourth inch slices of raw potatoes and heat gradually. When the fat ceases to bubble and the potatoes are well browned, strain through cheesecloth, cover and keep in a cool place. A small amount of fat may be clarified by adding to the cold fat, boiling water. Stir vigorously and set aside to cool; the fat will form a cake on the top, and may be easily removed. The sediment will be found on the bottom of the cake, and can be scraped off with a knife.

TO RENDER FAT (BEEF, GOOSE OR DUCK FAT).

Cut the fat into small pieces. Put in a deep iron kettle and cover with cold water.. Place on the stove uncovered; when the water has nearly all evaporated, set the kettle back and let the fat try out slowly. When the fat is still and scraps are shriveled and crisp at the bottom of the kettle, strain the fat through a cloth into a stone crock, cover and set it away in a cool place.

TO RENDER BUTTER.

Any butter that is unfit for table use may be made sweet and good for cooking purposes and will last for months, if prepared in the following manner: Place the butter in a deep iron kettle, filling only half full to prevent boiling over. Set it on the fire where it will simmer slowly for several hours. Watch carefully that it does not boil over, and when the fat is clear, and the sediment at the bottom is just browning, take it from the fire gently, so as not to disturb the sediment. Let cool a little, strain through cloth into crock, cover, and keep in a cool place.

DOUGHNUTS.

1 pint flour,	¼ teaspoon cinnamon,
½ pint sugar,	A little grated nutmeg,
1 teaspoon salt,	2 tablespoons melted
2 teaspoons baking pow- der,	butter,
	½ cup milk,
	1 egg.

Sift dry ingredients. Add the milk to the beaten egg, and combine the mixtures. Roll on well floured board, cut with form, or roll into small balls, and fry in deep fat. Dust with powdered sugar.

DOUGHNUTS.

3 eggs,	1 teaspoon soda,
1 cup sour cream,	4 cups flour,
	A little grated nutmeg.

Beat eggs, add sugar gradually and stir again. Add soda to cream. Combine the two mixtures and add the flour. Roll quite thin, cut or shape into form and fry in deep fat. Dust with powdered sugar.

FRIED POTATO BISCUITS.

Take one cupful of flour, one cupful of cold mashed potato, one ounce of compressed yeast dissolved in a little lukewarm milk and one-fourth teaspoon of salt sifted into the flour; mix all together and add rich milk enough to make like biscuit dough; roll out about one-half inch thick; cut into two-inch squares, let rise, and fry a golden brown in deep, smoking hot fat.

CRULLERS OR SNOWBALLS.

1 egg,	1 tablespoon cream,
1 tablespoon sugar,	¼ teaspoon salt,
1 teaspoon butter,	1 teaspoon brandy,
	Flour to roll.

Mix butter, salt and sugar with the egg. Add the cream and brandy and flour to make a stiff dough. Toss on a floured board and roll very thin, in pieces three inches long by two inches wide. Make four one inch gashes with a knife at equal intervals. Run fork in and out of gashes and lower into the deep hot fat. Fry until light brown and sprinkle with powdered sugar.

HESTERLISTE.

3 eggs, well beaten,	2 teaspoons baking pow-
5 tablespoons melted	der.
butter,	Flour to roll.
1 pint milk,	

Flour enough to roll as thin as pie crust. Cut into strips and fry in hot lard.

GERMAN PANCAKES.

1 pint flour,	3 eggs, whites separate.
1 pint milk,	

Heat butter in deep sauce pan so as to boil, drop a large spoonful of the batter into hot butter and fry quickly. Rub up the edges of the pancake as it fries, and turn over; drain on butchers' paper and serve with lemon and sugar.

POTATO PANCAKES.

6 raw grated potatoes,	1 teaspoon salt,
3 whole eggs,	1 tablespoon flour,
A pinch of baking powder.	A little milk.

Beat eggs well and mix with the rest of the ingredients. Drop by spoonfuls on a hot buttered spider, in small cakes. Turn and brown on both sides.

MATZOS PANCAKES.

8 eggs, beaten separately.	½ teaspoon salt,
½ cup matzos flour,	Sugar to taste.
1 lemon (juice and rind),	6 cold boiled potatoes,
	grated.

Mix batter evenly and lastly add the beaten whites of the eggs. Fry in small cakes in hot goose fat or butter. Serve with stewed prunes.

CORN FRITTERS.

Boil and pare four ears of corn, add salt, pepper, one cup flour, two eggs, and one-half pint cold milk. Stir vigorously, but do not beat. When firm, fry until brown on both sides in a buttered pan.

FRITTERS.

1 egg,	1 tablespoon melted
¼ cup water or milk,	butter,
	⅛ teaspoon salt,
	½ cup flour.

Beat the yolk and the white of the egg separately. To the yolk add the butter and salt and one-half of the liquid, and stir in the flour to make a smooth dough. Add the remainder of the liquid gradually to make a batter, and beat in the stiff white of the egg. Fry in deep, hot fat. The fritters may be served with syrup, with sugar and cinnamon, or with pudding sauce.

To make Apple Fritters, add one teaspoonful of sugar to the batter. Cut cored apples into slices (in rounds), dip in the batter and fry them. Sprinkle them with sugar and cinnamon before serving.

PINEAPPLE FRITTERS.

Soak the slices of pineapple in white wine or any liquor you have, with a little sugar added, for an hour before using. Fry in batter, as you would apple fritters.

FRITTERS SOUFFLE.

¼ pt. boiling milk,	1 oz. butter.
Vanilla,	

Mix the above and add half a cup sifted flour and stir until it forms a paste, then boil. Remove from fire and place into another vessel. Add two tablespoons powdered sugar, two yolks, pinch salt, the beaten white of one egg, one-half tablespoon whipped cream. Roll on a floured board. Sprinkle with flour, cut size of a walnut and fry in hot lard.

CHAPTER VII.

CEREALS.

DIGESTION OF FOODS.

All food is changed into a liquid before it can be carried about by the blood, to build up the worn out tissues.

Digestion: First Step—In the mouth, the food is crushed and some of the starch is changed to sugar by the saliva.

Second Step—In the stomach, the gastric juice dissolves the proteids.

Third Step—Through the agency of the bile, pancreatic and intestinal juices:

(a) The rest of the starch is changed to sugar.
(b) The rest of the proteids are dissolved.
(c) The fat is divided into small globules.

COMPOSITION OF CEREALS.

	Proteid.	Fat.	Starch.	Mineral Matter.	Water.
Oatmeal	15.6	7.3	68.0	1.9	7.2
Cornmeal	8.9	2.2	75.1	.9	12.9
Entire Wheat Flour	14.2	1.9	70.6	1.2	12.1
Rice	7.8	.04	79.4	.4	12.4
Pearl Barley	9.3	1.0	77.6	1.3	10.8

GENERAL RULES.

Boiling water and salt should always be added to cereals—one teaspoon salt to one cup of cereal.

They should be cooked directly over heat the first five minutes and then over boiling water in a double boiler.

Long cooking improves the flavor and makes them more easily digested.

Any cooked cereal or mush may be poured into a small greased bread pan, or one which has been wet in cold water; when cold, cut into one-third inch slices, dipped into flour, and browned in a little fat.

Gruels:—Any cold mush that is thinned with cream, milk or water and served very hot, is a gruel.

Gruels must be thoroughly cooked, strained, seasoned and served very hot.

They are flavored with sugar, stick cinnamon, whole cloves, meat extracts and stimulants.

ROLLED OATS OR WHEAT.

1 cup meal,	2 cups boiling water,
	1 teaspoon salt.

Boil ten minutes, stirring constantly; then over boiling water one hour longer. A better flavor is developed by longer cooking. One-fourth pound of dates, stoned and cut in pieces and stirred in the mush, may be added.

CORNMEAL MUSH.

4 cups boiling water,	1 teaspoon salt,
	1 cup cornmeal.

Boil ten minutes, stirring constantly; then over boiling water three hours longer.

FRIED MUSHES.

Where mushes are cooked to fry, use less water in steaming and add a little flour. Pack in greased bread pan or baking powder can; cover, which prevents crust from forming. The next morning, remove from can, slice thinly, dip in flour, cook until crisp, and brown in a little hot fat. Serve with syrup.

BAKED CORN CAKE.

1 pint cornmeal,	1 oz. butter.
2 quarts boiling water,	2 teaspoons salt.

Scald and salt. Spread about one-fourth inch thick on baking pan; finish in hot oven till quite dry.

FRIED CORN CAKES.

1 pint of cornmeal,	1 oz. butter.
1½ pints boiling water,	2 teaspoons salt.

Scald and salt. Make up in cakes about three inches across and one-half inch thick. Fry on each side till crusty.

CRACKER GRUEL.

4 tablespoons powdered cracker crumbs,	1 cup boiling water,
	1 cup milk,
	½ teaspoon salt.

Boil up once and serve.

STEAMED RICE.

1 cup rice,	3 cups boiling water,
	1 teaspoon salt.

Wash the rice and add to it the boiling salted water. Steam in double boiler twenty minutes, or until the rice is tender. Stir with a fork.

To wash rice: Place rice in strainer over cold water and rub and wash between hands, changing the water until it is clean. A variety of dishes made of rice may be obtained by steaming with three times the bulk either with water, milk, the two together, stewed tomatoes, soup stock, etc., but always added boiling hot.

CHAPTER VIII.

EGGS AND OMELETS

COMPOSITION OF EGGS.

Proteids, 14.9%. Mineral matter, 1%.
Fat, 10.6%. Water, 73.5%.

GENERAL RULES.

A stale egg rises in water; fresh eggs are heavy, and sink to the bottom. Wash eggs as soon as they come from the store. Eggs should never be boiled, as that renders them tough and difficult of digestion. They should be cooked just under the boiling point.

SOFT COOKED EGGS.

Have the water boiling, drop in the eggs gently, and place on stove where they will not boil, but only simmer, for from five to eight minutes.

HARD COOKED EGGS.

Place the eggs in boiling water, move to a warm place, where they will not boil, only simmer, and let cook thirty minutes.

EGG VERMICELLI.

4 hard cooked eggs, 6 to 8 slices toast,
2 cups white sauce.

Separate the yolk and white of egg and chop the white. Put the yolk in a warm place. Make a white sauce. Add the whites to the sauce. Heat thoroughly, and pour the mixture upon the toast. Press the yolk over the whole, through a fine strainer, and garnish with toast points and parsley.

WHITE SAUCE.

2 tablespoons butter,	¼ teaspoon pepper,
2 tablespoons flour,	1 teaspoon salt,
	2 cups hot milk.

Melt butter in a saucepan. Remove from fire and mix with flour. Add the hot milk gradually and boil, stirring constantly until the mixture thickens. Season and serve hot.

CURRIED EGGS.

Peel six hard cooked eggs and slice them. Put into a frying pan one teaspoon butter and one teaspoon chopped onion and stir until brown. Add two tablespoons flour and one-half teaspoon curry powder, one cup hot milk, salt, pepper. Simmer until the onions are soft, then add eggs. Garnish with bread croutons.

STEAMED EGGS.

Break an egg into a buttered cup. Sprinkle it with salt and pepper. Put into a steamer and cook until the white is set (three to five minutes). Remove carefully from cup with teaspoon. Serve on toast garnished with toast points.

POACHED EGGS.

Break each egg into a saucer; slip the egg into boiling water, and remove to cooler part of the stove. Dip the water over the eggs with a spoon, when the white is firm and a film has formed over the yolk, the egg is cooked. Take up with a skimmer, and drain and serve on slices of toast. Season.

CREAMY OMELET.

4 eggs,	½ teaspoon salt,
4 tablespoons milk,	⅛ teaspoon pepper,
or water.	1 teaspoon butter.

Beat eggs slightly, enough to blend the yolks and whites. Add milk and seasoning. Put butter in hot spider; when melted, turn in the mixture. As it cooks, draw the edges toward the center with a knife until the whole is set. If desired brown underneath, place on hotter part of the stove. Fold and turn on hot platter.

FOAMY OMELET.

2 eggs,	1 teaspoon butter,
2 tablespoons milk,	⅛ teaspoon salt,
or water.	White pepper or cayenne.

Beat the yolks until light and creamy. Add seasoning and milk; beat whites until stiff but not dry, and cut them into the yolks. Heat a spider, and with a knife rub it all over with butter, and turn in the omelet; spread it evenly on the pan and cook until it sets. Dry slightly on top in oven for a few minutes. Fold and serve immediately.

OMELET WITH WHITE SAUCE.

½ tablespoon butter,	¼ cup milk,
½ tablespoon flour,	1 egg,
⅛ tablespoon salt,	½ teaspoon butter (for
Pepper,	pan),

Make a white sauce of the first five ingredients. Separate yolk and white of egg and beat them until light. When the sauce is cool, add the yolk and cut in the white. Turn on heated buttered pan and cook until set.

OMELET WITH FLOUR.

3 eggs, beaten separately,	2 tablespoons flour,
1 cup milk,	½ teaspoon salt.

Stir one-quarter of the milk with the flour and salt mixed, until smooth, add the rest of the milk and pour and stir over the beaten yolks, then fold in whites, beaten dry. Pour in a hot buttered spider and cook slowly on top of stove five minutes, set in a moderately slow oven and bake twenty minutes more or until set and a golden brown. Fold and serve on hot platter.

BREAD OMELET.

2 tablespoons bread	2 tablespoons milk,
crumbs,	1 egg,
1 speck of salt.	½ teaspoon butter.
1 speck of pepper.	

Soak the bread crumbs in the milk for fifteen minutes, then add the salt and pepper. Separate the yolk and white of the egg and beat until light. Add the

yolk to the bread and milk and cut in the white.
Turn in the heated buttered pan and cook until set.
Fold and turn on heated dish.

ORANGE OMELET.

Rind of ⅛ orange,	1 tablespoon orange juice,
1 egg,	2 tablespoons powdered sugar.

Beat the yolk of the egg and add the orange rind and
juice. Add the sugar. Fold in the beaten white and
turn on heated buttered pan and cook until set. Serve
with powdered sugar.

CHAPTER IX.

SOUPS

Long soaking in cold water draws out the juices of meat and dissolves the gelatine. Soup stocks are prepared in this manner and then cooked at a low temperature.

BEEF JUICE No. 1.

Select a piece of steak from the rump or upper part of round. Broil or warm slightly one or two minutes, to set free the juices, then squeeze out the juice by means of a press or lemon squeezer, into a slightly warmed cup. Salt if necessary, and serve at once. Prepare only enough to serve, as it does not keep well.

BEEF JUICE No. 2.

Scrape one-half pound lean, juicy beef to a fine pulp. Put it into a double-boiler, with cold water in the lower part, heat gradually, and keep it simmering 1 hour, or until the meat is white. Strain and press out the juice, season with salt to taste, and serve hot.

BEEF TEA.

Shred one-half pound lean, juicy beef, and place it in a double boiler, with one cup of cold water and one-half teaspoon salt. Let it stand one hour. Then put boiling water in the lower part of boiler and cook five or ten minutes, until the juice is brown. Strain and press the meat to obtain all the juice. Serve hot, salt to taste.

SOUP STOCK.

2 lbs. soup meat, fat and bone,	1 small onion,
	½ small carrot,
2 qts. cold water,	1 piece celery root,
	2 teaspoons salt.

Prepare and season the meat as usual, cut it into small pieces. Put it into the cold water and let stand one-half hour. Simmer five hours; then add the vegetables cut fine, and the seasoning. Cook one-half hour longer. Strain and cool. When ready to use, remove the cake of fat, bring the stock to a boil, adding more salt if necessary.

Serve with noodles, barley, peas, rice, etc.

VEGETABLE SOUP.

1 cup soup stock,	1 tablespoon onion
1 tablespoon turnip,	(chopped),
1 tablespoon carrot,	1 potato (diced),
	¼ teaspoon salt.

Scrape the carrot, peel the onion and the turnip, removing the thick skin; cut all in small cubes; cook until nearly tender in boiling water, add the potatoes and salt, and when done the boiling soup stock. Other vegetables may be added.

BEEF SOUP.

Cover two and one-half pounds of short ribs of beef and a small piece of beef liver with two and one-half quarts of cold water. Add a tablespoonful of salt and put all on to boil at once. Remove scum only once when the meat has begun to boil, as too frequent skimming detracts from its strength. Let it simmer for one hour before putting in the vegetables. Then add a large tomato and a few shreds of cabbage, a medium sized onion, a large carrot and a piece of parsley and celery root, sliced. The celery root may be omitted if you have saved the green tops of your table celery for this purpose, a handful being sufficient. Let your soup simmer slowly for three hours or more until the meat is tender and ready to fall apart. Then strain through a fine sieve, and skim the fat which has settled at the top. Season at once with pepper, adding more salt if desired. If you require more soup add a little hot water at once before the stock begins to cool and gelatinize.

MULLIGATAWNY SOUP.

½ raw chicken, cut into pieces,
¼ green pepper,
¼ oz. raw dried beef,
½ green apple cut into pieces,
½ onion, sliced,
1 qt. soup stock,
1 teaspoon curry powder,
2 tablespoons rice,
Salt and pepper.

Brown the chicken, beef, onion and green pepper in a sauce pan, add the soup stock and the rest of the ingredients. Season with salt and pepper to taste. Boil one hour. Add twelve oysters two minutes before serving.

POTATO SOUP.

3 potatoes (cut small),
2 teaspoons chopped onions,
½ teaspoon salt,
1 quart boiling water,
⅛ teaspoon white pepper,
2 teaspoons chopped celery,
2 teaspoons parsley (chopped fine),
2 tablespoons butter,
1 tablespoon flour.

Heat one tablespoon butter, add the onions and celery, and let simmer ten minutes. Add potato, cover, and cook two minutes. Add the water and boil one hour. Add more boiling water as it evaporates. Bind the remaining flour and butter, add some potato liquid and cook. Combine the mixture and serve hot with the croutons.

TOMATO SOUP.

1 can or quart of tomatoes,
1 pint of water,
4 cloves,
1 slice of onion,
2 teaspoons sugar,
1 teaspoon salt,
⅛ teaspoon soda,
2 tablespoons butter,
2 tablespoons flour.

Cook the first six ingredients twenty minutes; strain, add the soda, melt the butter, add the flour, and gradually the hot strained tomatoes.

SPLIT PEA SOUP.

Soak one pint of split peas over night in cold water. Wash, drain, and simmer in three pints of water, stirring often with a wooden spoon and adding more water as evaporation takes place. When the peas begin to grow tender, add an onion and four or five stalks of celery, cut fine and sautéd in a little dripping, (that from the top of a dish of stock preferred). When all are tender, press through a purée sieve, reheat, and stir into the boiling soup three tablespoonsful, each, of flour and butter, creamed together and diluted with a little of the soup to a smooth paste. Let simmer ten minutes. Serve with croutons. Smoked meat may be cooked with the peas if desired.

CREAM OF POTATO SOUP.

3 potatoes,	⅛ teaspoon white pepper,
1 teaspoon salt,	2 teaspoons parsley,
2 teaspoons chopped	1 pint milk, or
onions,	1 pint milk and water,
Celery salt,	mixed,
1 tablespoon flour,	1 tablespoon butter.

Cook the potatoes until soft, drain; cook the milk and onion in a double boiler. Beat the potatoes with wire potato masher; add the hot liquid and strain, and return to the double boiler; make a white sauce, using this liquid. Cook five minutes and add the chopped parsley.

CREAM OF ASPARAGUS.

2 ounces butter,	Chopped parsley,
3 tablespoons flour,	2 bunches green aspara-
3 pints stock,	gus,
	½ cup of cream.

Drain and rinse asparagus, reserve tips and add stalks to cold water. Boil five minutes, drain, add soup stock and one slice onion. Boil thirty minutes, rub through a sieve. Heat butter and flour and the seasoning and cook with the hot stock and milk. Serve with the tips and croutons.

CREAM OF TOMATO SOUP.

½ can or pint of toma-
  toes,
¼ teaspoon soda,
1 slice onion,
1 teaspoon salt,
2 teaspoons sugar,

¼ teaspoon white pepper,
2 tablespoons flour,
2 tablespoons butter,
1 quart milk or milk and
  water mixed.

Cook the onion with the milk. Heat butter, add flour and seasoning, and the hot milk gradually. Heat the strained tomatoes, add the soda, and when the bubbling stops, add the tomato to the white sauce.

CREAM OF BARLEY OR RICE.

1 cup barley,
1 qt. stock,

1 onion,
Salt and pepper.

Boil forty-five minutes, strain and serve with thickening made of one cup hot cream stirred into two beaten yolks of eggs, add a handful of croutons.

CRABFISH CREAM SOUP.

Take the crab meat out of the tails of twelve crabs (or crawfish), dry the shells and pound them together in a mortar; add one ounce butter, place on fire until it clarifies (about five minutes), strain, add crab meat and cayenne pepper to taste. Scald one quart milk, add above prepared crab meat, one cup cream and flour to thicken.

OYSTER STEW.

Wash one pint oysters by adding one-quarter cup cold water. Pick over the oysters. Scald the milk, add one tablespoon butter, salt and pepper. Add the oysters and cook until plump and the edges curl. They should not be allowed to boil.

CREAM OF OYSTER SOUP.

Wash oysters with one-half cup of cold water through colander, reserving the liquid, heat gradually to the boiling point, parboil oysters, drain and skim the liquid. Make a white sauce, melting two tablespoons butter, adding two tablespoons flour, the hot strained liquid, salt and pepper to taste, and cook until smooth. Add the oysters and serve with oyster crackers.

FARINA BALLS.

1 cup hot milk,	1 teaspoon butter,
¼ cup farnia,	2 eggs.

Put the butter into the hot milk, add farina and stir it on the stove. Add eggs and stir. Cool and roll into marbles. Boil them in the soup just before serving.

CRACKER OR MATZOS BALLS.

Butter size of walnut,	Chopped parsley,
1 egg,	Salt and cracker meal.

Stir the butter, add egg, then as much cracker meal as it absorbs. Moisten with a little soup, add parsley and salt. Roll into marbles and boil in the soup just before serving.

NOODLES.

2 eggs,	Flour to make a very stiff
½ teaspoon salt,	dough.

Beat the eggs slightly, add salt and the flour gradually. Knead until dough is smooth and quite stiff. Roll very thin. Cover with a towel and set aside to dry about twenty minutes. Fold the dough, or cut into broad strips lengthwise and then into very fine strips crosswise, if wanted for soup. Or about one-half inch wide, if wanted as a vegetable. They may be dried and kept in a jar, covered with cheese-cloth.

CHAPTER X.

FISH.

COMPOSITION OF FISH.

	Refuse.	Proteid.	Fat.	Mineral Matter.	Water.
Black Bass	54.8	9.3	.8	.5	34.6
Whitefish	53.5	10.3	3.0	.7	32.5
Herring	42.6	10.9	3.9	.8	41.7
Trout	48.1	9.8	1.1	.6	40.4
Perch	62.5	7.2	1.5	.4	28.4
Pickerel	47.1	9.8	.2	.7	42.2

GENERAL RULE.

Fish is less stimulating and nourishing than the meat of other animals, but is easier of digestion. Fresh fish have firm flesh, plump eyes, and bright red gills. To scale fish, use fish-scaler or knife. Begin at the tail end and go toward head, slanting the knife toward you to prevent scales from flying. Rinse and cleanse thoroughly in cold water. Sprinkle fish with salt and pepper, to preserve it and improve the flavor.

TO BONE A FISH.

Clean the fish thoroughly. Beginning at the neck, on the inner side of fish, cut with a sharp knife, the bones on one side, close to the backbone. Cut down to the tail close to the backbone, so the fish will lay flat on the board.

Scrape flesh from bone with back of knife, removing in one piece the backbone and bones attached. Remove bones from other side with knife and pick out remaining small bones. Take care not to break the outer skin.

FRIED FISH.

Clean fish, wipe dry as possible, sprinkle with salt and pepper, dip in flour, crumbs, or cornmeal, then in egg and again in crumbs. Let stand a few moments. Then fry a golden brown in deep hot fat.

SAUTED FISH.

Clean fish, sprinkle with salt and pepper, dip in flour or cornmeal, and cook in spider with enough hot fat to prevent its sticking to the pan. Shake the pan occasionally. Brown well on under side, then turn and brown on the other side.

BROILED FISH.

Clean the fish. Split a thin fish down the back, and if you prefer, cut off the head and tail. Cut thick fish into slices and remove skin and bone. Oily fish need only salt and pepper, but dry fish should be spread with a little butter before broiling. Use double wire broiler and grease it. Put the thickest edge of the fish next to the middle of the broiler and broil the flesh side first. Cook about eight to twelve minutes, or until a delicate brown. Move the broiler up and down, that all parts may be equally browned, and then turn and cook the other side to crisp the skin. Broil over a clean fire, or if gas stove is used, one inch from gas in hot broiling oven. When done, the fish should be white and firm, and separate easily from the bone. Remove to a hot platter, flesh side up, first loosening fish from broiler. Spread with salt, pepper and butter, and garnish with slices of lemon and parsley.

PLANKED FISH.

Fish is planked when baked on a board (hickory, oak or ash) in the oven. Place the board in oven until very hot. Place the fish on board, season with salt and pepper and a little butter, or split it and place it skin down on the board; brush with butter and dust with salt and pepper. Baste often with melted butter, and bake until a golden brown. Serve with parsley, lemon or pickles sliced. Whitefish is best served in this style.

BAKED FISH.

Baked fish is prepared same as planked fish, but baked on a greased tin sheet in a dripping pan until a golden brown, basting often. If a raw sliced tomato or some canned tomatoes be placed on the top of the fish when half done, the flavor will be improved.

BOILED FISH.

3 lbs. fish, cut in slices and sprinkled with salt,
1 qt. water,
1 tablespoon carrot, cut fine,
¼ teaspoon whole pepper,
1 tablespoon onion, cut fine,
1 tablespoon celery, cut fine.

Clean fish and let stand in salt several hours. Let the water, pepper and vegetables boil until the water is well flavored. Add the fish, a few slices at a time, and let simmer until the flesh is firm and leaves the bones, no matter how long the time. Place on platter. Strain and reserve the fish stock, if wanted. Trout is nice if served this way, with a mayonnaise dressing.

SOUR FISH.

Cook the fish in water seasoned with salt, celery, one onion, one carrot, whole peppers, cloves and one tablespoon vinegar. When the fish is done, drain it and make sauce as follows: Soak four ginger snaps, one-half cup brown sugar and one-fourth cup vinegar, add to this a cup of the water the fish was boiled in, lemon slices and raisins, and boil until smooth. It must taste strong of vinegar and sugar, and more of either may be added to suit taste.

FILLED FISH.

Clean the fish thoroughly, remove the skin without breaking, and the flesh by scraping it from the bones. Begin at the neck. With care, the backbone may be removed with all of the small bones at-

tached. Chop the flesh fine, add to a three-pound
fish: one onion, medium size (chopped); salt and
pepper to taste; a few bay leaves, one-half · cup
bread or cracker crumbs, a little sugar, if desired;
one egg; one tablespoon chopped almonds. Mix
these ingredients well. Wash fish-skin, and fill with
the mixture. Sew up with coarse thread; shape, and
place in gently boiling vegetable stock. Boil slowly
until the stock is nearly absorbed.

BAKED FISH WITH SARDELLES.

Take a trout, split it as for broiling and remove
center bone. Place on a buttered platter, skin side
down, cover with one-half cup butter, one cup thick
sour cream, one-fourth pound sardelles which have
been soaked in water and chopped fine, cayenne pepper, a little cracker dust. Bake in hot oven one-half
hour. Serve on small platter.

PICKLED HERRING.

6 milk herring,	A few pepper corns,
2 medium sized sour ap-	½ oz. chopped almonds,
ples, chopped fine,	4 bay leaves,
1 large onion, sliced,	1½ cups vinegar.
1 tablespoon sugar,	

Soak herring in cold water twelve hours. Clean well,
bone and drain. Reserve the milk glands, mash them
well, mix, and strain with sugar and vinegar. Place
in jar in layers, herring, chopped apples, sliced onions, almonds, pepper, bay leaves, and pour on the
vinegar to cover. Cover jar and keep in a cool, dry
place. Almonds and apples may be omitted.

SAUCES FOR FISH AND MEAT.

LEMON SAUCE FOR FISH No. 1.

2 lemons, juice and rind.	1 teaspoon sugar.
2 yolks of eggs.	Salt to taste.
1 cup of hot fish stock.	Chopped parsley.

Stir the grated rind of the lemons with the well-beaten yolks, add the juice and very gradually pour on the hot fish stock. Cook until thick, stirring constantly. Add the sugar and parsley. Serve with fish, cooked in boiling water, to which salt, onion, whole pepper, parsley and a tablespoon of lemon juice has been added.

The sauce may be made thicker by cooking a teaspoon of cornstarch (wet in cold water) with the strained fish stock, or more yolks of eggs may be added.

LEMON SAUCE FOR FISH No. 2.

Juice of one large lemon, one-fourth pound butter, pepper and salt. Heat, but do not allow to boil. Then mix it with two well beaten yolks.

"SHARFE" FISH SAUCE.

1 tablespoon butter,	1 cup hot fish stock,
1 tablespoon flour,	1 egg (yolk).

Melt the butter, add the flour and the hot fish stock. Take from fire and pour very gradually on the beaten yolk. Pour while hot over the boiled fish. Garnish with parsley.

FISH SAUCE WITH MAYONNAISE.

2 cups water,	4 eggs (yolks),
2 tablespoons chopped almonds (blanched),	2 tablespoons sugar,
2 lemons (juice),	1 tablespoon flour or cornstarch,
2 tablespoons seeded raisins,	1 teaspoon salt.

Boil water, lemon juice, chopped almonds and raisins until almonds are soft; add gradually the sugar and cornstarch wet in a little cold water and boil; add very gradually to the well beaten yolks of four eggs. Take from stove and when cold, add mayonnaise dressing to taste. Serve with cold boiled fish garnished with capers, olives or chopped pickles.

MAYONNAISE DRESSING.

Yolks of 4 eggs,	1 tablespoon mustard,
¾ cup vinegar,	⅛ teaspoon red pepper,
¼ cup water,	1 tablespoon flour,
3 tablespoons sugar,	1 teaspoon salt.
1 tablespoon butter,	

Mix the dry ingredients, then add the butter, vinegar and water; boil over hot water until thick, then pour gradually to the beaten yolks. When ready to serve add a little cream or lemon juice to thin.

SAUCE MAITRE D'HOTEL.

One ounce butter in a bowl with a teaspoonful chopped parsley, juice of one-half lemon. Stir well. Keep in a cool place until wanted, and then heat it.

SAUCE HOLLANDAISE.

½ cup butter,	2 yolks,
½ cup hot water,	½ lemon (juice),
	Salt and pepper.

Cream the butter, add eggs and seasoning, and just before serving, add hot water. Stir it all up in a double boiler until it is thick.

TARTARE SAUCE No. 1.

Chop very fine a small onion, twelve capers. Place these in an earthen bowl with one-half teaspoonful dry English mustard, two raw yolks, one-quarter teaspoonful salt, and one-eighth teaspoonful pepper. Pour in very lightly one cupful good olive oil.

TARTARE SAUCE No. 2.

1 teaspoon mustard,	½ cup of oil,
⅛ teaspoon pepper,	3 tablespoons vinegar,
1 teaspoon powdered sugar,	1 tablespoon chopped olives,
¼ teaspoon salt,	1 tablespoon capers,
Few drops of onion juice,	1 tablespoon pickles,
	2 yolks.

Mix in the order given, add the yolks and stir well. Add the oil slowly, then vinegar and chopped ingredients. Will keep for several weeks.

SAUCE BEARNAISE DELMONICO.

Chop one small onion or one-fourth garlic. Place it in a small sauce pan on hot stove, two tablespoonfuls tarragon vinegar, four whole crushed peppers. Reduce until nearly dry, and put away to cool. Mix with it six yolks, stirring briskly, add gradually one and one-half ounce good butter, salt and a little cayenne.

Put the sauce pan into a large one that has boiling water in it, thoroughly heat it, and stir hard. When the sauce is firm, add one tablespoon strong soup stock. Strain all and serve hot with meat.

TOMATO SAUCE.

Melt one tablespoon of drippings, butter or fat, in a sauce pan. Cook in it one level tablespoon finely chopped onion until a golden brown, then add one tablespoon flour and add by degrees one cup of hot meat stock or boiling water, and one-half cup strained tomatoes; add one tablespoon sugar, one-half teaspoon salt, a speck of ground cloves, pepper. Let it cook thoroughly and serve with fish or meat.

WHITE SAUCE.

2 tablespoons butter,	¼ teaspoon pepper,
2 tablespoons flour,	½ teaspoon salt,
	1 cup hot milk.

Melt butter in a saucepan. Remove from fire and mix with flour. Add the hot milk gradually and boil, stirring constantly until the mixture thickens. Season and serve hot.

NOTE—Double quantities of flour for sauce in making croquettes.

HORSERADISH SAUCE FOR SOUP MEAT.

Two tablespoons grated horseradish, three-fourths pint white cream sauce, salt, red pepper, and a little sugar. Stir well on hot fire, add a little vinegar and one-half cup cream.

FRICASSEE SAUCE.

Stir gradually into a bowl, three beaten yolks, one-half pint of white sauce. Put them into a jar and stand in a basin of boiling water, and stir until it thickens. Just before serving, add juice of half a lemon.

CHICKEN, MADEIRA SAUCE.

Cut chicken as for fricassee, brown it in butter and add a little soup stock or water, one small onion sliced, one teaspoon paprika, salt, mushrooms and a wineglass of Madeira. Cook two and one-half hours.

SAUCE ALLEMANDE.

2 cups thick white sauce,
½ tablespoon lemon juice,
1 yolk of egg.

Add the hot sauce to the beaten yolk gradually, heat until thick, stirring constantly, then add the lemon juice.

MINT SAUCE.

¼ cup chopped mint   1 tablespoon powdered
  leaves,   sugar.
½ cup vinegar,

Add sugar to vinegar; when dissolved pour over mint and let stand thirty minutes over slow fire to infuse. If vinegar is strong dilute with water. Serve with lamb.

CHAPTER XI.

MEAT.

GENERAL RULES.

Meat should be removed from the paper in which it is wrapped and kept in a cool place.

The fibres of the meat contain nearly all the proteids (albumen).

Soaking meat in cold water draws out the blood, dissolves part of the organic salts, the soluble albumen and the extractives or flavoring matters.

Boiling water hardens albumen on the outside, keeping in the juice.

Intense heat, as in boiling, roasting or pan broiling, does the same thing.

Cooking under the boiling point after the first ten minutes, causes the toughest meat to become tender.

Meat is said to be "kosher" when the animal from which it is taken has been cut in the throat (not knocked in the head), the blood allowed to flow out that it may not coagulate. Before using, to further draw out the blood, it is soaked one-half hour in cold water, then allowed to stand one hour in salt, and then rinsed in cold water.

POT ROAST.

2½ pounds of beef (chuck),	1 onion, chopped fine,
1 tablespoon drippings,	1 pint boiling water,
	1 tablespoon flour,
	Salt and pepper.

Season and prepare meat as desired, and sprinkle over with flour. Heat the fat and fry the onion in it until light brown; add the meat, brown on all sides to harden the albumen to keep in the juices. Pour on the boiling water, and then let simmer slowly until tender. Add a little boiling water to prevent burning. Sliced or stewed tomato laid on top of the meat one-half hour before serving, makes a fine flavor. Thicken the gravy with one tablespoon flour and pour all around the meat. Serve with Franconia potatoes.

ROAST BEEF.

Prepare and season meat as desired. Dredge with flour. Place on rack in dripping pan, with two or three tablespoons of fat, in a hot oven, that the surface may be quickly seared, thus preventing escape of its juice. Reduce the heat and baste every ten minutes with the fat that has fried out. When meat is about half done, turn it over, dredge with flour, finish browning. If necessary, add a small quantity of water. Allow fifteen to twenty minutes for each pound of meat.

PAN-BROILED CHOPS.

Prepare meat and salt as desired. Have a frying pan very hot, without any fat, put in the chops and cook one minute, turn and sear the other side, to harden the albumen, and keep in the juices; then cook more slowly until done. Stand them up on the fat edge to brown the fat, without over cooking the meat. Serve hot, either plain, with tomato sauce or with peas.

NOTE—Steak is nice prepared this way.

SCRAPED BEEF.

Cut a piece of tender steak one-half inch thick. Lay it on a meat board and with a sharp knife scrape off the soft part until there is nothing left but the tough, stringy fibres. Season the pulp with salt and pepper, make into little flat round cakes one-half inch thick, and broil them two minutes. Serve on rounds of toast. This is a safe and dainty way to prepare steak for one who is just beginning to eat meat. When it is not convenient to have glowing coals, these meat cakes may be broiled in a very hot frying pan, or in the broiling oven of a gas stove.

HAMBURG STEAK.

1 lb. round steak,	1 teaspoon chopped
1 tablespoon drip-	onions,
pings,	Salt and pepper.

Take one pound of raw flank or round steak. Salt and prepare as desired. Cut off fat, bone and stringy pieces. Chop it very fine. Chop onions very fine and mix with meat. Season to taste. Make into round cakes a little less than one-half inch thick. Have ready a frying pan with the drippings; when hot, put in the steak and cook brown. Serve hot on hot platter, and garnish with celery tops or parsley, and two or three slices of lemon on meat. Pour the fat that the steak was cooked in over the meat.

BEEF LOAF.

1 lb. round steak, chop-	Salt and pepper,
ped,	½ cup bread crumbs,
1 teaspoon chopped	½ cup cold water.
onions,	

Mix in the order given and bake in hot oven in small greased bread pan until done and nicely browned.

BROILED STEAK.

Prepare meat as desired; wipe, trim off extra fat. Grease the broiler with some of the fat. Broil over a clean fire or in broiling oven of gas stove, turning every ten seconds to sear meat and retain the juices. Cook three or four minutes if liked rare; longer, if well done. The steak should be one inch thick. Serve hot.

STEAK FOR THE OVEN.

Sirloin steak about two inches thick. Put in pan, salt it, add two tablespoons Worcestershire sauce, and three tablespoons catsup and little lumps of butter over the top. Put in hot oven for twenty minutes.

STEAK IN CASSEROLE.

Broil a thick steak a few minutes; then put it into a casserole. Add one carrot, one onion, one par-

sley sprig, one bay leaf, one-half turnip, one teaspoon catsup, six mushrooms, one wineglass Madeira wine. Let cook slowly until vegetables are
tender.

FILLET OF BEEF.

Lard a four-pound fillet, season with salt and pepper, put it into a roasting pan and roast thirty minutes
in hot oven. Garnish with vegetables.

BROILED TENDERLOIN.

Three pounds tenderloin cut into three or four
pieces. Flatten a little, season with salt, pepper, a little sweet oil and broil. Serve with sauce Bearnaise;
or, if preferred, melted butter.

BRAISED BEEF.

A piece of rump weighing three pounds, larded.
Season with salt, pepper, chopped parsley and garlic.
Add one carrot, cut into round pieces; one slice
onion, one bay leaf. Cover and brown well on both
sides. Baste it often and add a little soup stock.
Brown and strain the gravy over the meat.

STEWED MUTTON.

Prepare and season to taste, remove the pink skin
and extra fat, and put into boiling water. Boil fifteen
minutes, push kettle back, and allow the meat to cook
slowly until tender fifteen minutes for each pound. A
carrot, diced and cooked with the meat, improves the
flavor. Serve meat with a border of baking powder
biscuits, split in halves, and pour all over the top the
following gravy: (Any tough meat is nice prepared
in this way.)

Gravy for Mutton: To each cup of meat stock,
add one tablespoon flour, moistened with a little
cold water, and stir until smooth and thick like
cream, pour it slowly into the boiling stock, stirring
all the time. Boil until thoroughly cooked. Add
salt and pepper to taste, and just before serving, add
one teaspoon chopped parsley.

VEAL.

Veal is meat from the calf, and is less nourishing than beef or mutton. The muscle should be pink or flesh colored, and the fat white and clear. Veal should be thoroughly cooked, to make it digestible. Spring is the season for veal. It is cooked and served the same as other meats.

VEAL CUTLETS.

Use slices one-half inch thick. Wipe and season. Dip in egg, then in cracker or bread crumbs. Fry slowly until well browned, in a little hot fat.

GULASH.

Veal and beef mixed. Cut into one inch squares and brown in hot fat with one onion, salt and one heaping teaspoonful paprika. When the meat is brown, add one cup strained tomatoes, and one-half hour before serving, add some small potatoes.

MOCK BIRDS.

Take veal steak, cut thin, three by five inches in size, fill with chopped boiled ham, a small lump of butter, salt, pepper, chopped parsley and a little chopped onion. Make little rolls of them and tie or pin with a tooth pick. Brown them well in hot butter. Add a little soup stock and flour and boil. Add one cup sour cream shortly before serving.

MOCK ROAST DUCK.

Make a dressing of bread, seasoned as for chicken and moisten. Take two large slices from round of veal, three pounds. Salt the meat, cut out the bones, and close the holes with two or three stitches. Sew the edges together to hold the stuffing securely, making a smooth, oval body.

Rub three ounces each, of butter and flour to a cream, and with a knife spread evenly over the form, except where it touches the pan. Put one-half a cup of water in the pan with the roll, and bake in a moderate oven about one hour, or until thoroughly done. The crust should be a golden brown, like a roasted duck. Remove carefully from the pan to platter, so as not to break the crust.

NOTE—Flank steak may be prepared the same way.

WARMED-OVER MEATS.

ROAST BEEF WITH GRAVY.

Cut cold roast beef in thin slices, place on a warm platter and pour over some of the gravy reheated to the boiling point. If the meat is allowed to stand in gravy, it becomes hard and tough.

POTATO AND MEAT PIE.

Chop cold meat fine, removing the bones, fat and gristle. Put the meat in a pudding dish. To each cup of meat, pour in one-third cup of gravy or one-fourth cup water. Taste, and stir in, if needed, one-fourth teaspoon salt, one speck pepper, and a few drops of onion juice or a little chopped parsley. Spread mashed potatoes as a crust over the meat, bake on the grate of the oven, until golden brown.

HASH.

Chop the meat as in the preceding recipe. To each cup of meat, add two cups of potatoes (mashed or chopped), one-half teaspoon salt, and a speck of pepper. Mix thoroughly. Put two tablespoons boiling water into a frying pan. Add one tablespoon butter or dripping, and the hash and let it cook slowly, until browned on the bottom. Do not stir. Fold over and turn on a hot platter. A little stewed tomato or onion juice may be added.

CASSEROLE OF RICE AND MEAT.

Steam
{
1 cup rice,
3 cups boiling water,
1 teaspoon salt,

2 cups cold cooked meat,
½ teaspoon salt,
¼ teaspoon celery salt,
⅛ teaspoon pepper,
⅛ teaspoon poultry seasoning,

1 teaspoon chopped onions,
2 tablespoons cracker crumbs,
1 egg,
1 cup hot water or stock.

Steam the rice twenty minutes. Chop the meat very fine, add all seasonings, then the beaten egg, cracker crumbs, and stock, or hot water enough to pack it easily. Line the bottom and sides of a greased mould or small bread tin one-half inch thick with the cooked rice, pack in the meat, cover closely with rice, then cover with greased paper and steam forty-five minutes. Loosen around the edge of mould, turn out upon a hot platter and pour tomato sauce around it.

RISSOULES.

2 cups cooked meat,
¼ cup hot water or meat stock,
⅛ teaspoon salt,
2 tablespoons cracker crumbs,

1 teaspoon onion, (chopped),
¼ teaspoon celery salt,
⅛ teaspoon pepper,
1 egg.

Can use any cold cooked meats. Cut the meat off the bones, remove fat, gristle and skin; put the meat in a chopping bowl and chop very fine, season it with salt, pepper, and a little chopped onion or celery salt. Add half as much bread crumbs as you have meat, moisten with a well beaten egg or eggs, or use a little thickened gravy, form into small cakes or a loaf. Put into shallow pans with a little beef drippings over the top; bake in a moderate oven about thirty minutes, a delicate brown. Serve with tomato sauce or a thickened gravy.

CROQUETTES.

Chop cold cooked meat into small pieces, add sea· soning to taste—salt, cayenne pepper, chopped parsley; add a thick white sauce and cool. Shape into cylinders and cover with crumbs, egg, and again with crumbs. Cook in deep fat until brown.

SCALLOPED MEAT.

2 cups cold meat (cooked).	1 egg,
1½ teaspoons salt,	3 tablespoons fat,
¼ teaspoon pepper,	3 tablespoons flour,
¼ teaspoon onion juice, or	1½ cups hot meat stock,
parsley,	2 cups bread or cracker crumbs.

Make sauce with the fat, flour and seasoning, and add the hot stock gradually. Put one-half of the crumbs in a baking dish. Pour sauce mixed with meat (cut in small pieces) in dish, cover with crumbs and brown in oven twenty minutes.

CHICKEN A LA WALDORF.

Cut white meat of boiled chicken into dice. Two truffles cut into dice, put into a sauce pan with one pint cream, salt, pepper, and boil twelve minutes. Pour gradually on two beaten yolks diluted in two large spoons of Madeira wine. Cook until it thickens, stirring constantly.

POULTRY.

Poultry includes chickens or fowls, turkeys, ducks and geese. The flesh of poultry is lighter in color than that of animals, but it is very nourishing. Fowls may be stewed, chickens roasted or broiled.

Singe chicken by holding it over blazing paper. Remove pin feathers with the point of a knife. The internal organs should be removed as soon as killed. Make an opening at the vent, or under one of the legs, and remove them, taking care that the gall bladder, near the liver, is not broken. Remove the windpipe and pull the crop out from the end of the neck, remove the oil-bag from the tail. Take out lungs and kidneys. Press the heart to extract any blood. Take off the inner coat of gizzard; this, with the heart and liver, are called giblets. Wash chicken with cold water.

ROAST CHICKEN.

Dress, clean and season chicken. Place it on its back in a dripping pan, with two tablespoons fat. Dredge with flour and place in hot oven. When the flour is well browned, reduce the heat, then baste every ten minutes, adding a little water when necessary to prevent burning. Turn chicken frequently. When the breast meat is tender, it is done. A four-pound chicken requires one and one-half hours.

STUFFING FOR POULTRY.

Place pieces of stale bread in cheese cloth bag or cloth, soak in tepid water, and squeeze. Take out of bag; add pepper, salt and ginger to taste, and a little melted fat. Mix thoroughly, and add a beaten egg and a little onion if you wish.

CHESTNUT STUFFING.

Shake one quart of large chestnuts, in each of which a gash has been cut in the shell, in a tablespoon of melted butter, then set in the oven five or ten minutes. Remove the shells and inner skin together, and cook until tender in boiling salted water. Drain and pass through a ricer. Add one-fourth a cup of butter, one teaspoonful of salt, a dash of pepper, a pint of bread crumbs moistened with one-fourth a cup of butter, and additional seasonings, as onion or lemon juice and chopped parsley, according to taste. If a moist dressing be preferred, add cream or stock.

GRAVY FOR ROAST CHICKEN.

Pour off the liquid from pan in which the chicken has been roasted. Skim off four tablespoons fat, add four tablespoons flour to it, brown and add two cups stock, in which the giblets were cooked. Cook five minutes. Season with salt and pepper and add the giblets, chopped fine.

BIRDS EN CASSEROLE.

6 squabs,	1 onion,
1 sprig parsley,	4 cloves,
1 bay leaf,	12 mushrooms,
½ carrot,	½ wineglass sherry,
1 pt. soup stock,	1 tablespoon catsup.

Place in the casserole, parsley, bay leaf, onion; then the squabs or chicken; add soup, salt, pepper or paprika; cover the dish and put into the oven one and one-half hours. Baste every fifteen minutes. When tender, make sauce as follows: Put into a sauce pan one tablespoon butter, one tablespoon flour. When light brown, strain and add the sauce from the birds; when boiling, remove from the fire and add wine, mushrooms and catsup. Pour all over the birds, return to the fire, and when hot, serve in the casserole.

STUFFING FOR SQUABS.

If the squabs or pigeons are stuffed with a bread stuffing, add to it a few spoonfuls of sherry. It gives a dainty taste to the forcemeat, quite unlike anything else.

An orange sauce is delicious with fried or roasted squabs. In the pan in which they were roasted, make a plain gravy with flour and water. Then add a tablespoonful of chopped parsley, two tablespoonsful of orange juice, the grated rind of an orange, and salt and pepper as necessary. Strain, and serve hot. If the squabs are broiled, make a gravy the same way in a sauce-pan, and add a tablespoonful of meat essence, and flavor the same way.

PICKLED MEAT.

10 lbs. beef,	¾ tablespoon saltpetre,
1 cup brown sugar,	Salt and pepper to taste.
¼ tablespoon powdered wash soda,	

Place in a stone jar, cover with large soup plate and allow to draw juice over night. Then cover with cold water and leave in this brine ten days. Tongue or goose-meat may be pickled in the same manner.

SMOKED GOOSE.

Remove wings, legs and the skin of the neck of a goose, take off the remaining skin and fat and reserve the fat for rendering. Separate the breast and back, remove internal organs, and clean all parts thoroughly. Pickle the meat as directed in the foregoing recipe. When pickled, take out the breast and legs, and leave them whole, scrape the meat carefully from the rest of the bones, removing all tendons and tissues, and chop very fine. Now pack this chopped meat into the skin of neck and sew up with coarse thread. Have the legs, breast and neck smoked, and serve cold, sliced thin.

TO PRESERVE GOOSE MEAT.

If goose is too fat to roast, remove and cut the skin into small pieces and render or try out the fat. The scraps, when brown, shriveled and crisp, are called "Greben," and are served hot or cold. When fat is nearly done or clear, add the breast and legs of goose, previously salted, and boil in the fat until tender and browned. Place meat in crock and pour the clear hot fat over it to cover. Cool. Cover crock with plate and stone and keep in a cool, dry place. Will keep for months. When ready to serve, take out meat, heat, and drain off fat.

HASEN PFEFFER.

Lay the rabbit meat in a jar and cover with vinegar and water, equal parts; one sliced onion, salt, pepper, cloves and bay leaves. Allow this to soak two days. Remove the meat and brown it thoroughly in hot butter, turning it often, and gradually add the sauce in which it was pickled, as much as is required. Before serving, stir one cupful thick sour cream into the sauce. Beef may be prepared the same way.

CHAPTER XII.

VEGETABLES.

Vegetables are chiefly valuable for their potash salts. They contain much cellulose, which gives needed bulk to the food. Dried peas, beans and lentils may be used in place of flesh food since they contain a large amount of proteid. They should be soaked in cold water over night to freshen and boiled several hours to soften in salted water.

Starch is found in most vegetables and grains. It is a fine, glistening powder; each grain, studied microscopically, is found to be covered with a thin skin.

By experiment with cornstarch, we find:

1. Cold water simply separates the starch grains.
2. Boiling water bursts the thin skin on the outside of the grains and dissolves the starch.
3. Starchy foods should be cooked in boiling salted water.
4. Water boils when the bubbles come to the top and burst.

COMPOSITION OF POTATOES.

Water, 78%.	Mineral matter, .9%.
Starch, 18%.	Fat, .1%.
Proteids, 2.1%.	

Potatoes should be eaten with fish, meat or eggs, as they lack proteids and give needed bulk rather than nourishment. They should be kept in a cool, dry cellar. When sprouts appear, they should be removed.

BOILED POTATOES.

6 potatoes,	1 qt. boiling water,
	1 tablespoon salt.

Scrub, pare, and cover with cold water. Cook in boiling salted water twenty to thirty minutes, or till tender. Drain and shake gently over the fire uncovered, till dry. Serve hot.

MASHED POTATOES.

6 hot boiled potatoes,	Pepper, and enough milk
2 tablespoons butter,	to moisten,
	½ teaspoon salt.

Rub the hot potatoes through a ricer, or mash and add the rest of the ingredients in their order. Beat with a fork until light and creamy. Serve hot.

NOTE—Any kind of fat may be used and the milk omitted. An onion may be chopped fine and browned in the fat and poured over the potatoes.

BAKED POTATOES.

Take even sized potatoes. Scrub and cut out black portions. Place on floor of hot oven until soft, thirty to forty minutes. Break the skins to let the steam escape. Serve at once uncovered. Peel at once any that may be left.

NOTE—Sweet potatoes are baked the same way, but may be parboiled before baking.

POTATO BALLS.

Pare potato and throw into pan of cold water. With French cutter, cut balls, or cut into cubes and let stand in cold salted water until wanted. Scraps may be used for soup or mashed potatoes. Heat one tablespoon butter in a saucepan, add the potato balls, cover closely and cook slowly, shaking pan over fire to cook them evenly. Test with darning needle. When ready to serve, add one teaspoon salt and one teaspoon chopped parsley to one pint potato balls, or they may be boiled, drained and hot butter and chopped parsley added.

BOSTON BROWNED POTATOES.

Wash and peel six medium sized potatoes. Cut in four equal parts. Place in a shallow tin, greased, and bake one-half to three-fourths of an hour in a hot oven. When done, pour over some meat gravy, and serve alone or around the meat on a hot platter. Serve at once.

FRANCONIA POTATOES.

Wash, scrub and pare potatoes of uniform size. Put them in the dripping pan with the meat and baste when the meat is basted. Or place in a small tin pan beside the meat, or on the grate, and baste with the drippings.

SARATOGA POTATOES.

Pare and slice potatoes very fine. Soak in cold salted water, and drain dry between towels; fry only a handful at a time in clear, hot fat, until a delicate brown and crisp. Drain on unglazed paper. Sprinkle with salt and serve hot or cold.

FRENCH FRIED POTATOES.

Pare, wash and cut lengthwise into eighths. Soak in cold salted water. Drain and dry, and fry in clear, hot fat, until tender and golden brown.

WARMED-OVER POTATOES.

DUCHESSE POTATOES.

Mash five nicely boiled potatoes until fine, add one tablespoon of butter, two tablespoons of cream, pepper and salt to taste, and yolk of one egg. Press through a pastry bag on greased tin in form of meringues. Brush with beaten egg and brown in oven.

LYONNAISE POTATOES.

1 pint cold boiled sliced potatoes,	Pepper,
½ teaspoon salt,	2 tablespoons fat,
1 teaspoon chopped onion,	2 tablespoons chopped parsley.

Season sliced potatoes with pepper and salt. Fry the onions-light brown in the fat, put in the potatoes and cook till it has taken up the fat. Add the chopped parsley and serve.

SCALLOPED POTATOES.

1 quart cold boiled potatoes,	1 cup buttered cracker crumbs,
1 teaspoon salt,	4 tablespoons chopped parsley.
¼ teaspoon pepper,	
1 cup white sauce,	

Slice potatoes, season with salt and pepper and parsley. Butter a baking dish. put in the potatoes, pour on the white sauce, cover with crumbs and bake until brown; or take raw sliced potatoes, season with salt, pepper and add bits of butter, cover with milk or cream and bake until the milk is evaporated.

SURPRISE BALLS.

Roll mashed potatoes into balls, and press a hollow in the top with a teaspoon. Chop and season cold, lean meat, and put one teaspoon into the hollow of the potato ball. Put a little fat on the top of each ball, and brown in the oven.

POTATO CAKES.

Take cold mashed potatoes and make into round cakes, one-half inch thick. Put them in a hot greased frying pan, fry well on one side until golden brown, then turn over and brown the other side.

POTATO PUFFS No. 1.

Take two cupfuls of cold mashed potatoes, stir into it six teaspoonsful melted butter, beating all to a cream; then add two eggs, whipped stiff, and a teacupful of cream or milk, salting to taste; beat all well, pour into a deep dish and bake in a quick oven until brown.

POTATO PUFFS No. 2.

2 cups grated, boiled potatoes,	1 cup flour, Salt.

Sour cream enough to make it possible to knead the mixture. Roll it out thin as you can and cut with biscuit cutter. Fry in hot lard.

ONIONS, CARROTS, CABBAGE, ETC.

Wash thoroughly, pare or scrape. Stand in cold water. Cook in boiling water, and keep at the boiling point. Use one teaspoon salt with one quart water. Add salt when vegetables are partially cooked. The water in which vegetables are cooked is called vegetable stock.

Cabbage, cauliflower, onions and turnips should be cooked uncovered in a large amount of water. Peel onions under cold water. All vegetables must be drained as soon as tender. Cold boiled vegetables may be used as salads, or may be placed in a baking dish with one-half the quantity of sauce (two cups vegetables to one cup sauce) covered with buttered crumbs and browned in a hot oven.

BOILED GREEN CORN—ON COB.

Pare off the outer leaves, boil in water, add one-half cup milk, one-half ounce butter, and salt.

FLEMISH CARROTS.

Scrape and slice sufficient new carrots to measure one quart. Put them in a sauce pan with one teaspoonful of salt, cover with boiling water and boil for fifteen minutes. In a stewpan put two tablespoonfuls of butter and one button onion chopped fine, and cook slowly for five minutes; add the drained carrots, one teaspoonful of sugar, one teaspoonful of salt, one-quarter of a teaspoonful of white pepper, and shake over the fire for ten minutes; add one and one-half cupfuls of good stock, cover and simmer for half an hour. Add one teaspoonful of finely chopped parsley, taste to see that the seasoning is quite right, and serve.

ASPARAGUS.

Cut asparagus on lower parts of stalks as far down as they will snap. Wash, remove scales and retie bunches. Cook in boiling salted water fifteen minutes, or until tender, leaving tips out of water first ten minutes. Drain, remove string and add white sauce, or pour over them a few bread crumbs browned in hot butter or fat, allowing one tablespoon butter to one bunch asparagus.

ASPARAGUS HOLLANDAISE.

Boil the asparagus twenty minutes in salted water, and pour the following Hollandaise sauce over it, just as you send it to the table.

Sauce: Heat one-half cup butter, one-half cup water and juice of one-half lemon, stir in the yolks of two eggs, gradually add salt and pepper. Cook until thick.

ARTICHOKE SAUTES.

Cut six fine green artichokes into quarters and remove the chokes. Trim the leaves neatly and parboil them five minutes in salted water, drain. Lay them in a sautoire, season with salt, pepper and two ounces butter. Cover and cook in a moderate oven twenty-five minutes. Serve with any desired sauce. Hollandaise, as in the above recipe, is best.

STEWED TOMATOES.

Wipe and cover tomatoes with boiling water. Let stand one minute, then skin. Cut in pieces, put in stewpan, and cook slowly twenty minutes, stirring occasionally. Season with butter, salt, pepper and a little sugar, if desired; add some bread crumbs.

STUFFED TOMATOES.

Wash and dry six tomatoes. Cut the top of each off without detaching, so that it will serve as a cover. Scoop out the inside, chop one small onion, place in a sauce pan with one-half ounce butter, six chopped mushrooms and one ounce sausage meat or chopped chicken meat, salt, pepper, the scooped tomato, one-half cup fresh bread crumbs and chopped parsley. Mix and cook well, and fill tomatoes, place on platter over hot water, cover with buttered paper and bake.

MUSHROOM SAUTES.

One pound mushrooms. Pare, wash and drain, place in a spider with one ounce of butter, salt and pepper. Cover and cook ten minutes, tossing them. Add juice of one-half lemon, and chopped parsley. Serve on hot toast.

BROILED MUSHROOMS.

Pare, wash and dry one pound fine large mushrooms. Lay them on a dish, season with salt, pepper and one teaspoonful of sweet oil. Roll them well, broil four or five minutes on both sides; arrange them on toast, and pour melted butter over them.

BAKED ONIONS.

Select even sized onions, wipe, but do not peel. Place in baking dish, roots down, and bake one hour, or until tender. Remove from fire, remove roots, peel carefully, return to dish, add pepper, salt, and a little melted butter or other fat; let stand five minutes in oven, and then serve hot.

CHESTNUT VEGETABLE.

Peel and blanch one pound of large chestnuts. Then boil very slowly in water until about half done; drain off any remaining water and add one cup of soup stock and one cup of sugar. Let this simmer until it is soft, adding also butter size of walnut. Serve in ramikins.

BAKED BEANS.

Let a pint of pea beans soak in cold water over night. Wash, rinse, and parboil, until the beans can be easily pierced with a needle, adding one teaspoonful of soda. Rinse in hot water. Put one-half the beans in the bean pot, then one-fourth a pound of dried beef. Add the rest of the beans, and over them· pour one teaspoonful each of mustard and salt, and a scant fourth a cup of molasses, mixed with sufficient hot water to cover. Bake about eight hours in a slow oven, keeping the beans covered with water and the lid on until the last hour. Then remove the lid, and brown the beans.

CAULIFLOWER.

Select cauliflower with white head and fresh, green leaves. Remove leaves, cut off stalk and soak (head down) in cold water. Separate flowerets and cook twenty minutes or until soft in boiling water. Drain and reheat in one and one-half cups of white sauce.

STRING BEANS.

Wash beans, remove strings and cut in one inch pieces. Cook in boiling water until tender, from one to three hours. Add salt last half hour of cooking. Drain and add salt, pepper and butter, or make the following sauce: Two tablespoons butter, melt and add two tablespoons flour; then one cup of hot liquid in which the beans were cooked; add salt and pepper to taste, one tablespoon vinegar and one tablespoon sugar and cook until smooth and clear.

SPINACH.

Pick off the roots and the decayed leaves. Wash in three or four waters. Put the spinach in a large kettle, without water. Let cook slowly until some of the juice is drawn out, then boil a few minutes until tender. Drain and chop.

To one-half peck spinach take two tablespoons butter, heat, add one teaspoon chopped onion, fry a golden brown; add two tablespoons bread crumbs, one and one-half teaspoons salt, a little pepper, and then the spinach. Reheat and stir in two or more eggs and garnish with poached or hard cooked eggs.

SAUCES FOR VEGETABLES.

WHAT SAUCES CONTAIN:

Fat	Liquids	Seasoning
Butter,	Milk,	Salt,
Beef dripping,	Water,	Pepper,
Oil.	Milk and Water,	Spices,
	Vegetable stock,	Sugar,
Starch	with or without milk.	Flavoring extracts,
	Fish stock,	Wines,
Flour,	Meat stock,	Acids.
Corn Starch.	Fruit juices.	

WHITE SAUCE.

2 tablespoons butter,	¼ teaspoon pepper,
2 tablespoons flour,	½ teaspoon salt,
	1 cup hot milk.

Melt butter in a saucepan. Remove from fire and mix with flour. Add the hot milk gradually and boil, stirring constantly until the mixture thickens. Season and serve hot.

YELLOW CREAM SAUCE.

1 cup hot white sauce,	2 yolks of eggs.

Pour the white sauce gradually over the beaten yolks and cook slowly until thick, stirring constantly. Serve at once over cooked green peas, asparagus, etc.

BROWN VEGETABLE SAUCE.

2 cups vegetables.	1 cup liquid in which veg-
2 tablespoons butter,	etables were cooked or
2 tablespoons flour,	soup stock,
1 teaspoon salt,	White pepper.

Cut the vegetables in cubes and cook in freshly boiling water until tender, then drain and dry. Brown the butter, add the flour, brown, and seasoning, then gradually the hot water in which the vegetables were cooked, and cook until starchy taste is gone. If it gets lumpy, take from fire and beat until smooth. Put vegetables in the sauce and serve.

SWEET SOUR SAUCE.

2 tablespoons butter.	¼ teaspoon pepper,
2 tablespoons flour.	1 tablespoon vinegar.
½ teaspoon salt,	1 cup of hot vegetable
1 tablespoon sugar.	liquor or soup stock.

Brown butter well, add flour and brown seasoning, the hot liquid, vinegar and sugar to taste. Cook until smooth and serve as desired with cooked cabbage, string beans, etc.

CHAPTER XIII.

SALADS AND SALAD DRESSINGS.

GENERAL RULES.

The salad plants are valuable for the water and potash salts they contain. Lettuce, Endive, Watercress, and Cucumbers are examples. Salads are cooling, refreshing, and assist in stimulating the appetite. They should be served cold. An endless variety of salads are made of cooked meats (chicken, veal, sweetbreads, etc.), fish (canned or cold boiled), eggs, vegetables, raw (celery, tomatoes, cucumbers, etc.), or cooked (peas, beans, potatoes, asparagus etc.), fruits (bananas, oranges, apples, etc.) and nutmeats (English walnuts, pecans, boiled chestnuts, hickory nuts, etc.),alone or in combination—with the addition of a dressing. The salad greens should always be served crisp and cold, and the dressing added just before serving. Cooked vegetables and meats are best if marinated one hour before serving with salt and pepper, oil and vinegar, and boiled or mayonnaise dressing not added until ready to serve. All skin, bone and gristle should be freed from meat and fish, and cut in small cubes or flaked. Salads may be made very attractive by serving on lettuce leaves, in cups made by scooping out tomatoes, cucumbers, oranges, lemons, apples, etc.

FRENCH SALAD DRESSING No. 1.

½ teaspoon salt,
¼ teaspoon pepper,
2 tablespoons vinegar,
4 tablespoons olive oil or any poultry fat,
⅛ teaspoon onion juice.

Mix the ingredients, and stir until well blended. Used largely over lettuce, tomatoes, etc., and to marinate boiled meats and vegetables.

FRENCH SALAD DRESSING No. 2.

Chop in a bowl one-fourth onion, one-fourth green pepper, one branch parsley, one teaspoon salt, dash cayenne pepper, three tablespoons vinegar. Mix well and add slowly four tablesoons fine olive oil.

SOUR CREAM DRESSING FOR LETTUCE.

1 cup sour cream,   2 teaspoons sugar.

Beat together, add salt, pepper and vinegar to taste, and beat all together with a Dover beater until it thickens.

VINAIGRETTE DRESSING..

¼ chopped onion,	3 teaspoons vinegar,
2 branches parsley,	Salt and pepper,
8 stalks chives,	4 tablespoons good oil.

Mix all together but the oil; put that in last, and slowly.

BOILED DRESSING.

2 tablespoons flour,	1 egg or the yolks of 2,
½ teaspoon salt,	½ cup water,
3 tablespoons sugar,	½ cup vinegar,
¼ teaspoon celery salt,	1 tablespoon butter,
¼ teaspoon mustard,	1 cup cream whipped
Speck of cayenne pepper,	stiff.

Mix the first six ingredients, stir the egg in well. Add the vinegar and butter or the other fat, cook until well thickened in double boiler. This makes one cup of plain dressing. When ready to serve, one cup of cream whipped stiff is added to the plain dressing.

BOILED MAYONNAISE DRESSING

½ teaspoon mustard,	2 tablespoons vinegar,
¼ teaspoon salt,	2 tablespoons lemon juice,
1 teaspoon sugar,	1 teaspoon butter or other
Speck of cayenne pepper,	fat.
Yolks of 2 eggs,	

Mix the dry ingredients, add and stirr well with beaten yolks, then add the vinegar. Boil in double boiler until thick. Take from the stove, and add the butter or fat and the juice of the lemon. Thin with cream or lemon juice just before serving.

MAYONNAISE.

2 yolks,	1½ cups best oil,
¼ teaspoon dry mustard,	1 teaspoon vineagr,
3 dashes cayenne,	½ saltspoon salt.

Have mixing bowl and oil thoroughly chilled. Mix the dry ingredients, add egg yolks and when well mixed add one-half teaspoon vinegar; add oil gradually, at first drop by drop, stir constantly. As mixture thickens, thin with vinegar or lemon juice. Add oil and vinegar or lemon juice alternately until all is used, stirring and beating constantly.

SALAD DRESSING.

6 yolks,	2 tablespoons cream,
6 tablespoons oil,	1 lemon (juice),
2 tablespoons vinegar,	½ teaspoon mustard.

Salt and cayenne to taste. Mix all together and boil in a double boiler. Stir constantly till thick. If too thick when wanted, stir in some more cream.

DELMONICO SALAD DRESSING.

1 hard cooked egg, chopped fine,	2 tablespoons olive oil,
1 teaspoon tomato catsup,	¼ teaspoon chopped green peppers,
1 teaspoon Worcestershire Sauce,	Red pepper and salt to taste,
2 tablespoons tarragon vinegar,	Chopped truffles if desired.

TO MIX MUSTARD.

Take two tablespoons mustard and add to it gradually cold water or vinegar to make a smooth paste.

SALADS.

PLAIN POTATO SALAD.

1 qt. hot sliced potatoes,
1 medium sized onion
(chopped fine),

French dressing to moisten,
Parsley or 1 teaspoon chives (schnittlauch) cut fine, to garnish.

Boil potatoes in their jackets and while hot, peel and slice; add the onion, and mix with the French dressing. Garnish with parsley or chives.

POTATO SALAD.

1 qt. cold sliced potatoes,
1 medium onion cut fine,
1 cup table celery cut fine,

1 cup Boiled Dressing,
Pickles, beet, or hard cooked eggs to garnish.

Mix the first four ingredients together lightly and toss the dressing gently through it. Garnish as desired.

NOTE—If celery cannot be had, use chopped cab-. bage or pickles.

COLD SLAW OR CABBAGE SALAD.

1 cup red cabbage (chopped fine),

1 cup white cabbage (chopped fine),
1 cup hot Boiled Dressing.

Select nice firm red and white cabbage, wash, cut off wilted leaves, quarter and soak in cold water. Drain, cut into thin slices and chop very fine, each kind separately. Divide the dressing into two parts, mix with each part while hot. Take three-fourths of the white mixture, pack it smoothly on platter one inch from the edge. Make a wreath of the red all around the white, keeping the lines distinct and smooth. Reserve one-fourth of the red for a layer on the top of white and the remaining white to top the whole.

WATER LILY SALAD.

1 large or two small   3 to 6 eggs.
heads of lettuce,

Cook eggs one-half hour. When cold, remove the shell and cut the egg crosswise in small points to resemble leaves of a flower. Carefully wash and wipe the lettuce; cut the large leaves into narrow shreds, but save the nicest small ones whole. Then make a boiled dressing, arrange the finely shredded lettuce in the bottom of the platter, pour over it the dressing, arrange the leaves on top of it, put half an egg in the center of each leaf. Garnish with radishes.

CHESTNUT SALAD.

The chestnut salad is much in favor, and great is the variety both in method of preparation and serving. The chestnuts should in any case be cooked until very tender, cooled and mixed with French or mayonnaise dressing.

Equal parts of shredded celery and chestnuts is a popular combination.

Bananas, apples, celery and chestnuts go well together. The fruit is pared, cored and cut in slices and mixed with the chestnut meats. Dress with mayonnaise dressing and garnish with lettuce hearts.

WALDORF SALAD.

Cut two apples into dice and the same amount of celery, and cover with a mayonnaise.

VEGETABLE SALAD.

Cook beets, celery and onions, and slice them and pour French dressing over them.

PEPPER AND GRAPE FRUIT SALAD.

Remove the tops from six green peppers. Take out seeds and refill with grape-fruit pulp, fine-cut celery, and English walnut meats mixed with mayonnaise dressing. To one cup and a half of the mixture add one-fourth a cup of heavy cream, beaten stiff. For each pepper use three halves of walnut meats and half as much celery as grape-fruit.

SALAD OF PINEAPPLE AND CELERY.

Shred the pineapple, also the celery. Hollow out and peel apples, as many as you need; fill with the celery and pineapple, and cover with mayonnaise. Serve ice cold.

CELERY SALAD.

Hollow out green peppers and fill with chopped celery and chopped cabbage. Either mayonnaise or vinaigrette dressing can be used with it.

CELERY, CRESS AND WALNUTS.

Arrange on a round platter, cress around the outside edge, then celery cut into dice, in the center a mound of walnut meats. Mayonnaise or vinaigrette dressing.

HERRING SALAD.

3 herring, cleaned and picked to pieces,	1 pickle,
3 apples,	A little onion,
3 boiled potatoes,	A little pepper,
¼ cup mixed nuts,	A little sugar,
A little piece of cooked veal	A few capers,
	4 hard-boiled eggs.

Chop all fine, mix the yolks of the eggs with a little vinegar, and mix all together.

FRUIT SALAD.

3 oranges,	Sugar to taste,
3 bananas,	Juice of 1 lemon,
¼ lb. Malaga grapes,	12 English walnut meats.

Cut the oranges in two crosswise, reserving the peels as salad cups. Remove orange pulp separately from each section. Remove skins and seeds from grapes. Mix orange pulp and grapes, sprinkle with sugar, add lemon juice, and let stand in cool place several hours. Before serving, add the bananas sliced, and the walnut meats. Fill the orange shells with this mixture. One-fourth cup of wine may be added, if desired.

GRAPE FRUIT SALAD.

Remove from the skin the cells and juice; add a little sugar, chopped pineapple and a few Maraschino cherries. Serve very cold in thin glasses, surrounded with crushed ice, or in fruit shells.

FRUIT SALAD.

Alternate layers of sliced fruits, pineapple, bananas, oranges, grapes and some nut kernels. Pour over all wine dressing and chill one hour.

Wine Dressing: One-half cup of sugar, one-third cup sherry wine, and two tablespoons Madeira wine.

CHAPTER XIV.

ENTREES.
SCALLOPED DISHES AND CHAFING DISHES.

GENERAL RULES FOR SCALLOPED DISHES.

Bread crumbs for scalloped dishes are prepared by rubbing two pieces of stale bread together. They should be made from the inside of stale bread. They should be seasoned and the melted butter or fat added to them.

Place the food materials in two layers, using one-fourth amount of crumbs on the bottom of dish, one-fourth in the middle and the remaining one-half on the top.

More seasoning may be added.

Any cold cooked vegetable, meat, fish or fruit (raw or cooked) may be scalloped. Allow one cup of white sauce to two cups of vegetable.

Serve in pudding dish or individually in ramikins.

BAKED NOODLES WITH CHEESE.

Take the broad noodles, cook them in boiling salt water until they are soft. Drain through strainer, and pour cold water over them to prevent pieces from adhering. Make one and one-half cups white sauce.

2 tablespoons butter,	¼ teaspoon salt,
2 tablespoons flour,	1½ cups hot milk.

Dissolve a speck of soda in a little hot water and add to the milk.

Heat the butter, add the flour and seasoning, and then gradually the hot milk.

Put a layer of boiled noodles in a buttered baking dish, sprinkle with grated cheese; repeat, pour over white sauce, cover with buttered crumbs, and bake until crumbs are brown.

NOTE—Tomato sauce may be used in place of the white sauce and cheese.

SPAGHETTI ITALIENNE.

Boil the spaghetti in salt water, adding one-half ounce butter and a small onion. Add tomato sauce, Parmesan cheese, salt and cayenne pepper, and bake it until brown on top.

SCALLOPED OYSTERS.

1 pt. oysters,	½ cup stale bread crumbs,
4 tablespoons oyster liquor.	1 cup cracker crumbs.
	½ cup melted butter.
2 tablespoons milk or cream.	Salt,
	Pepper.

Mix bread and cracker crumbs, and stir in butter. Put a thin layer in bottom of buttered shallow baking dish, cover with oysters and sprinkle with salt and pepper; add one-half each of oyster liquor and cream. Repeat, cover top with remaining crumbs. Bake thirty minutes in hot oven. Never allow more than two layers for scalloped oysters; if three layers are used, the middle layer will be underdone.

SHRIMPS IN TOMATO CASES.

For one and one-half cups of shrimps, broken into small pieces, prepare six medium sized tomatoes by cutting in halves, removing the pulp, and inverting on a sieve to drain. Melt in saucepan two tablespoonfuls of butter, and cook in this, slowly, two slices of onion until slightly browned, then remove onion and add the tomato pulp. Cook this for fifteen minutes, and add a cup of stale bread crumbs and cream to make a soft paste, about one-fourth a cup. When well blended, add the shrimps, also high seasoning of salt and paprika, place in tomatoes, cover with buttered crumbs, and bake quickly until browned. Serve in lettuce leaves or on rounds of bread, either toasted or fried.

FILLET DE SOLE.

Two pounds flounder, boned and skinned and boiled in water, with salt, cayenne, onion, celery and carrot. Boil only a few minutes, drain, place in two long pieces on a well buttered platter with a space between. In this space put oysters or clams, some mushrooms, tomatoes strained, and plenty of butter and a little cracker dust. Bake twenty minutes.

LOBSTER IN SHELLS No. 1.

Cut into dice lobster and mushrooms (boiled), add yellow cream sauce, red pepper and salt. Put in shells, cover with cracker crumbs and butter and bake a light brown.

LOBSTER IN SHELLS No. 2.
(Deviled.)

Chop the boiled lobster and season with salt, red pepper, grated onion. Add one cup white cream sauce, and cook together three minutes. Fill the tail shell of the lobster with the above mixture, cover lightly with cracker dust and a little melted butter, and bake fifteen minutes.

LOBSTER FARCIE.
(In Ramikins.)

Chop the meat of the lobster, add salt, cayenne pepper and some soaked wheat bread. Heat one ounce butter, one-fourth onion, grated; add lobster mixture, one-half pint cream. Boil five minutes and bake in ramikins.

SHRIMP SPANISH.
(In Ramikins.)

1 pint shrimp,	1 cup hot soup stock,
1 tablespoon flour,	2 yolks,
1 tablespoon butter,	Salt, cayenne and grated
1 tablespoon catsup.	onion.
1 tablespoon cream,	

Heat butter, add flour, add other ingredients in order given. Cook until smooth and add the shrimps. Fill this mixture into ramikins and cover with cracker dust and butter, and bake.

SCALLOPED FISH.
(In Ramikins.)

Three pounds of boiled pike, pickerel or lake trout, boned, skinned and picked in small pieces. Boil fish until flesh leaves the bone in water with salt, cayenne, onion, celery and carrot, drain. Butter the ramikins, sprinkle with bread crumbs, put in a layer of the shredded fish, sprinkle with grated almonds and add another layer of fish. Cover with hot tomato sauce and sprinkle bread crumbs on top. Place ramikins in a pan of hot water and bake from fifteen to twenty minutes or until the crumbs are slightly browned. Serve hot, decorated with parsley.

CHEESE RAMIKINS.

4 tablespoons grated cheese,	Pepper and salt,
4 tablespoons grated bread,	½ cup cream,
2 tablespoons butter,	3 yolks,
	3 whites to froth.

Cook in a sauce pan until smooth, bread, cheese, butter and seasoning. Add yolk, then whites of egg. Grease the ramikins, fill three-fourths full and bake six minutes. Serve at once.

CHEESE FONDU.

Half a cup of bread crumbs, half a cup of dry cheese, grated, one scant cup milk, one tablespoonful of butter, one egg, yolk and white beaten separately, a speck of bicarbonate of soda, salt and pepper to taste. Soak crumbs in the milk, dissolve soda in a drop of hot water, and add to milk. Add rest of ingredients, beat well, pour into a well buttered baking-dish, strew dry crumbs moistened with butter over the top, and bake in a hot oven until light brown. Serve at once in the dish in which it is baked.

CHEESE SOUFFLE.

Two tablespoonfuls of flour, two tablespoonfuls of butter, four tablespoonfuls of grated cheese, four eggs, one pint of milk. Rub butter and flour together over the fire, when they bubble, add gradually hot milk;

season with pepper and salt. Add slowly the grated cheese. Add the beaten yolks, then the beaten whites, stirring all together thoroughly. Put in a pudding dish which has been well buttered, and bake in a moderately hot oven from fifteen to twenty minutes, until it is set —like custard.

CHICKEN TIMBALES.

Chop fine, and then pound half a pound of the white meat of a chicken from which the skin and sinews have been removed, add to this, while pounding, a rather scant pint of very cold cream, a little salt, white pepper, and the whites of five eggs, press through a sieve and then fill little tin moulds which have been well buttered, place them in a sauce pan in which you have put water about the depth of an inch. Cover the sauce pan, put into the oven for twenty minutes, then turn out of moulds on to a round platter, or serve individually with sauce allemande.

CHICKEN LIVER TIMBALES.

Eight chicken livers, chopped fine, strain through a sieve twice, then rub to a pulp. Add one tablespoon melted butter, two tablespoons rich cream, one table-spoon fine bread crumbs, salt and pepper, one teaspoon grated onion juice. Mix until smooth. Add yolks of two eggs, beaten white of one. Line the timball molds with butter first and then bread crumbs. Put in the mixture; bake in a pan half filled with water, for fifteen minutes. Serve at once with mushroom sauce. (The mixture must not stand after the eggs are put in, but bake at once.)

HALIBUT TIMBALE.

Take one-half pound uncooked halibut, cut it into fine pieces, pound it, put it through a strainer; mix a cupful of grated bread crumbs with one-half cup milk, stir to a smooth paste. Remove from fire, add the fish pulp, one-half teaspoonful of salt, a dash of red pepper; beat in lightly the stiff froth of five eggs. Fill the mould or moulds, place in a pan of hot water in the oven for twenty minutes. Serve with a Tartare or Hollandaise sauce.

FISH PUDDING WITH SAUCE HOLLANDAISE.

Two pounds of fish (raw)—halibut. One cup of cream, half pound butter, three eggs (froth the whites), two tablespoons of flour. Shred fish from skin and bone, chop fine, add cream slowly and pass through a fine sieve. Add other ingredients, whites last. Butter pudding mould, sprinkle with chopped parsley. Boil one and one half hours and serve hot with Sauce Hollandaise.

LOBSTER A LA NEWBURG.

The meat of two lobsters cut into one-inch pieces, placed into sauce pan with one ounce fresh butter, salt, cayenne pepper (two truffles cut into dice are a great improvement). Cook five minutes, add one wineglass Madeira, reduce to half by boiling three minutes.

Beat three yolks with one-half pint cream, and stir it into the above mixture. Shuffle lightly two minutes until all is blended, and serve on toast.

HALIBUT AND LOBSTER.

One and one-half pounds halibut boned and picked raw, chop fine, add salt, cayenne and beaten whites of five eggs, one cup of cream, whipped. Pack into a mould and boil thirty minutes. Serve in the center of a platter with lobster a la Newburg all around it.

LOBSTER CHOPS.

Chop the boiled meat of two large lobsters. Make a white cream sauce of one ounce butter, two tablespoons flour and one cup milk. Boil thoroughly, and add the lobster meat. Add a little grated onion, chopped parsley, salt and cayenne pepper. After cooking three minutes, remove from stove. Divide in heaps, about ten, on a piece of clean paper, and cool thoroughly. Form into chop shape, and roll in egg and then in grated bread crumbs. Fry in smoking hot fat. Serve with a claw in each, to represent the bone. Serve very hot, with Tartare sauce.

LOBSTER RISSOLES.

Mince the lobster meat, pound the coral and add it, grated onion, salt, cayenne. Add grated yolks of three hard-boiled eggs. Make a batter of two table-spoons milk, one tablespoon flour and one egg. Beat well together and mix the above with it. Roll into balls and fry.

BROILED LIVE LOBSTER.

Split the lobster and glaze with olive oil, broil on hot fire, with the meat side to the fire. When well broiled, season with salt, cayenne and plenty of melted butter, or place in spider, season, place in oven and baste.

SHRIMP A LA CREOLE IN CASSEROLE.

1 quart shrimps (boiled),	3 cloves,
½ can mushrooms,	1 bay leaf,
¼ can French peas,	2 tablespoons catsup,
¼ can tomatoes,	Salt and cayenne pepper.
1 onion,	

Stew all the above ingredients together, one hour in a casserole, adding the boiled shrimp cut into dice. Serve very hot.

EGG CUTLETS.

Put six eggs in a sauce pan, cover with cold water and simmer for an hour. Scald one pint of milk in a double boiler; rub together to a paste two tablespoon-fuls of butter and four tablespoonfuls of flour; turn this into the scalded milk and stir slowly until it dissolves and thickens. Cover and cook for five minutes, then season with one teaspoonful of salt, one-half of a tea-spoonful of paprika, a dash of cayene, one teaspoon-ful of onion juice and a pinch of mace. Take from the fire, add the hard-boiled eggs chopped rather coarsely, and one tablespoonful of chopped parsley. Spread out on a buttered dish and set away until cold. Dust the hands lightly with flour and shape spoonfuls of the mixture in small cutlets, being careful to pat them out until of an even thickness; use as little flour as possible, or the creamy consistency will be lost. When all are shaped, dip each cutlet into slightly beaten egg, then in fine dried bread crumbs, and immerse in smoking-hot fat until golden brown. Drain on unglazed paper and serve with tomato or cream sauce.

FRIED OYSTERS.

Clean, blanch and dry between towels, selected oysters. Season with salt and pepper, dip in flour, egg and cracker or stale bread crumbs, and fry in deep fat. Drain on brown paper, and serve hot. Garnish with parsley.

CHAFING DISHES.

The chafing dish is king, and everyone is looking for new recipes with which to regale and surprise his friends at the evening lunch.

It is said that the chafing dish originated with the Israelitish women, and that it has been used through each succeeding generation by both men and women.

For those who have plenty of money, there are little silver chafing dishes about four inches square, which are used for serving a rarebit or a bird individually. There is no lamp under this small dish, but there is hot water in the boiler, to keep the bird warm; of course it is cooked before it is placed in this small dish.

A tray should always be used under the chafing dish, as there is so much danger of setting fire to the tablecloth from the overflow of the alcohol, when no tray is used.

When a recipe calls for milk or cream, the hot water pan should be used in all cases, to avoid all possibility of burning; but when something is to be sauted, or fried, this pan is omitted and the dish is placed directly over the flame; constant watching and turning and shaking is necessary, however, as the alcohol flame is hot and comes in direct contact with the metal pan. Oysters are usually cooked in the blazer only, at first, and then, when they are plump, if a sauce is to be added to them, the hot water pan is introduced underneath.

WELSH RAREBIT No. 1.

1 tablespoon butter,	1 egg,
½ lb. cheese,	⅛ teaspoon salt,
¼ cup milk,	⅛ teaspoon mustard,
	Speck of cayenne pepper.

Melt the butter, break the cheese into small pieces, and add with the seasoning to the butter. When the cheese melts, add the egg, beaten with the milk, and cook one minute. Serve at once on toast or wafers.

WELSH RAREBIT No. 2.

1 lb. cheese cut into dice,	1½ teaspoons butter,
½ glass stale ale,	¼ teaspoon dry mustard,
	Salt and cayenne.

Put butter into the chafing dish; when melted, add cheese, mustard, salt and pepper, and gradually the ale or beer. Stir constantly. If desired, one teaspoon of Worcestershire sauce may be added.

CREAMED CRAB MEAT.

2 tablespoons butter,	1 cup cream,
½ cup bread crumbs,	½ teaspoon dry mustard.

Put the above into chafing dish; when it boils stir in crab meat, salt, cayenne or Tobasco sauce, and two beaten yolks. Serve at once.

LOBSTER A LA BORDELAISE.

One and one-half pounds lobster cut into pieces. Heat one glass red wine, one shallot chopped fine; also one small carrot; add lobster, salt, cayenne pepper and one-half pint of white sauce.

LOBSTER A LA THACKERAY.

Put into the sauce pan (or chafing dish) the green part of the lobster, and add one-fourth pound butter, one-fourth teaspoon salt, three dashes cayenne, one tablespoon walnut catsup, one teaspoonful paprika. Cook this five minutes, then add the meat of two lobsters cut into one-inch pieces.

CHICKEN A LA NEWBURG.

2 cups chopped chicken,	2 tablespoons butter,
1 cup cream,	Pepper and salt to taste.
Yolks of 3 eggs,	

Melt butter in chafing dish, add eggs, slightly beaten, and cream. Then add the chicken and a wineglass of sherry or Mareira wine.

OYSTERS A LA POULETTE.

30 oysters,	4 yolks,
1 tablespoon butter,	½ pint cream,
1 tablespoon flour,	Salt, cayenne,
1 cup bouillon,	Juice of ½ lemon.

Stir butter, flour and bouillon until well cooked and smooth, add seasoning and four yolks beaten with the cream. Steam thirty large oysters, pour sauce over them and cook two minutes; add chopped parsley.

FROG LEGS A LA NEWBURG.

Boil the frog legs in salt water and drain. Prepare sauce as follows:

1 oz. butter,	1 gill of Madeira,
	Salt and cayenne pepper.

Boil three minutes. Add one-half pint cream and three yolks. Cook two minutes, and pour over the frog legs.

NOTE—Frog legs are nice dipped in egg and cracker crumbs and fried a golden brown in hot fat.

CHAPTER XV.

CUSTARDS, PUDDINGS AND PUDDING SAUCES.

GENERAL RULES FOR CUSTARD.

Eggs should be thoroughly mixed with sugar and salt, add the hot milk slowly, stirring all the time. Custards must be cooked over moderate heat—over water in the oven if baked, or in a double boiler if steamed. When thick enough, the custard coats on the spoon. It curdles if cooked a minute too long. If it curdles, put in a pan of cold water immediately and beat until smooth. Always strain custards.

ORANGE CUSTARD.

1 pt. milk,	¼ cup sugar,
8 eggs,	½ teaspoon vanilla,
⅛ teaspoon salt,	3 oranges or 6 bananas.

Separate the yolks and whites of eggs. Beat yolks lightly, add the salt and sugar, and beat well. Pour the hot milk slowly into the eggs. Stir constantly until smooth and thick, and strain. When cool, flavor with vanilla. Peel and slice oranges or bananas, and place in serving dish. Pour on the custard, and take whites of the three eggs (beaten very light), one-fourth cup powdered sugar and few drops of vanilla for the meringue, and drop in large spoonfuls on the custard. Any kind of fruit may be substituted for oranges or bananas.

CHOCOLATE CUSTARD.

Follow the recipe for orange custard, melting one-half ounce chocolate with the milk.

CORNSTARCH MOULD.

One pint of milk, four tablespoonfuls of cornstarch, four teaspoonfuls of sugar, half a teaspoonful of flavoring, cocoa or one and one-half ounce melted chocolate, a speck of salt. Mix together the cornstarch and sugar with a little of the cold milk. Scald the remainder of the milk, and stir the moistened starch and sugar into it. Cook fifteen minutes in a double boiler. Add flavoring and salt, and pour at once into a cold wet mould. When cold, turn out and eat with stewed fruit, cream and sugar, or soft custard.

BAKED TAPIOCA PUDDING.

Cook one-fourth a cup of quick-cooking tapioca in a pint of milk until transparent. Add a few grains of salt, a tablespoonful of butter, half a cup of sugar, and remove from the fire. Let cool a little, then pour over one or two beaten eggs. Add a teaspoonful of vanila, and turn into a buttered baking-dish. Let bake in a very moderate oven until the egg is set. Three or four macaroons crumbled fine are an addition to this pudding. Serve hot or cold. If it be served cold, use from one-half to one whole cup of milk additional.

RENNET.

1 pt. milk,	1 tablespoon liquid rennet,
2 tablespons sugar,	or 1 tablet.

Heat the milk until lukewarm, add the sugar, and stir until the sugar is dissolved; add the rennet, and pour into a glass dish; leave until firm in a moderately warm place. Cool, and season with nutmeg or cinnamon. Serve with cream.

RICE PUDDING.

1 cup rice,	⅓ cup cup sugar,
3 cups boiling water,	1 tablespoon butter,
1 teaspoon salt,	1 egg (well beaten).

Steam the rice in the boiling salted water until tender, and while hot add the rest of the ingredients. Cook five minutes and bake twenty minutes in a buttered baking dish, with bread crumbs at the top and bottom. If desired, fruit may be added in layers to the rice.

RICE SNOW BALLS.

3 cups cooked rice,   ¼ cup sugar,
                       ¼ lb. stewed prunes.

Wring small pudding cloths, one-third yard square, out of hot water, and lay them over a one-half pint bowl. Spread the rice one-third of an inch thick over cloth. Put the stewed prunes in center, draw the cloth around until prunes are covered smoothly with the rice. Tie tightly and steam ten minutes. Remove cloth carefully and turn the balls out on a platter, and serve with prunes. This amount makes six balls. They may be filled with steamed apples or any other fruit.

BOILED CHOCOLATE PUDDING.

6 yolks,   1 teaspoon baking powder,
1 cup sugar,   6 whites, beaten stiff,
½ lb. grated chocolate,   Cinnamon, cloves, vanilla.
2 tablespoons cracker
  dust,

Boil in an absolutely air-tight pudding steamer one and one-half hours. Serve hot, with hard sauce.

NESSELROLE PUDDING.

1 cup cold water,   ⅔ cup raisins,
½ box Knox's gelatine,   8 tablespoons blanched
2 cups sweet milk,   almonds.
5 eggs,   Small piece of citron cut
                              fine.

Beat yolks of eggs with sugar and add to the hot milk. Cook one minute. Dissolve gelatine in the cold water. Add to milk mixture and cook again; then add the chopped nuts, raisins, citron and a little salt. When thickened remove from fire, stir well in a pan of cold water for almost five minutes. Then add the beaten whites of the five eggs. Also one tablespoon brandy and one tablespoon vanilla. Put in a mould until stiff. Serve with plain or whipped cream.

MACAROON CREAM.

Heat one pint of milk in double boiler; add mixture of one cup sugar and yolks five eggs; then add one-half box gelatine dissolved in one cup water. Cook until a little thick. Whip the whites till stiff, add to boiling mixture and mix well.

Pour brandy or rum into mold to wash it; line sides and bottom of mould with macaroons, pour in mixture, set aside to cool. Serve with or without cream.

ROTHE GRITSE.

One quart red raspberries, one quart red currants, put on to boil with two cups cold water. Strain and add one and one-half cups sugar. Let boil and add three heaping tablespoons cornstarch (which have been dissolved in cold water), when thick put in a melon mould and serve cold with cream.

FRUIT DESSERT.

1 pint raspberries,	1 lb. macaroons,
1 cup white wine,	Sugar.
6 eggs,	

Sweeten the raspberries and set aside. Beat the yolks of six eggs until light, stir them into the wine, sweetened and heated. Cook a few moments and set aside to cool. Place in dish a layer of macaroons, raspberries and wine custard alternately, until dish is full Beat whites to a stiff froth. Brown slightly in oven.

SCALLOPED APPLES.

3 cups apples, chopped,	¼ teaspoon nutmeg,
2 cups soft bread crumbs,	2 tablespoons butter,
½ cup sugar,	½ lemon, juice and rind,
¼ teaspoon cinnamon,	¼ cup water.

Melt the butter and add the crumbs; mix the sugar, spice and lemon rind. Put one-fourth of the crumbs in the bottom of a buttered dish. Then one-half of the apples. Sprinkle with one-half of the sugar and spice, then add another quarter of the crumbs, the remainder of the apples, and the sugar and spice. Sprinkle the lemon juice over this and the water, and put the rest of the crumbs over the top. Bake one and one-half hours, or until the apples are thoroughly cooked. Cover one hour.

NOTE—Scalloped Rhubarb is made the same way, adding more sugar and no lemon.

FIG PUDDING.

1 cup flour,	A pinch of salt,
2 teaspoons baking powder,	½ lb. dried figs,
	1 cup finely chopped beef
1 cup bread crumbs,	suet,
1 cup sugar,	2 eggs,
	1 cup milk.

Sift into a bowl the flour and baking powder, add the bread crumbs, sugar and salt, then the figs which must be cut up small, and the finely chopped suet. Mix all these dry ingredients well together before adding the eggs, which must be well beaten, and the milk. Turn into a greased pudding mould or bowl, cover closely and steam three hours. The pudding should be moist enough to pour easily into the mould.

APPLE SNOW.

2 apples (sour),	½ tablespoon lemon juice,
White of 1 egg,	1 tablespoon powdered
	sugar.

Pare, quarter and core two apples. Steam or cook in small amount of water until soft, and then rub through a sieve. Beat white of egg with wire spoon, add the sugar and the apple gradually. Pile lightly on glass dish and chill.

PRUNE WHIP.

Five whites of eggs, beaten very stiff, to which add one-half cup pulverized sugar and eighteen prunes, stewed and pressed through a ricer. Bake twenty minutes in a slow oven.

CHESTNUT FLAKE.

Blanch and boil chestnuts until half done in water, drain and put them into sugar syrup and boil until soft. Put through a potato ricer, and serve with whipped cream, flavored with maraschino.

CHOCOLATE SOUFFLE.

6 eggs—yolks,	1 cup sugar,
1 cup grated chocolate,	6 whites of eggs beaten.

Stir the yolks and sugar together, add the chocolate and six whites of eggs. Bake in a greased pudding dish, about fifteen minutes.

WALNUT SOUFFLE.

6 eggs—yolks,	1 cup grated walnut
6 whites of eggs, beaten,	meats,
	1 cup sugar.

Stir the yolks and sugar together, and then add the nuts and whites of eggs. Bake about fifteen minutes in a greased pudding dish.

LEMON SOUFFLE.

6 eggs—yolks,	6 whites of eggs, beaten
1 cup sugar,	very stiff.
3 grated lemons,	

Mix well and bake twenty minutes.

DATE PUDDING.

6 oz. of suet, chopped fine,	3 eggs, beaten separately,
6 oz. bread crumbs,	½ wineglass brandy,
6 oz. sugar,	½ or ¾ lb. stoned dates.

Beat the sugar and eggs together, stir in the other ingredients and steam two hours.

BAKED CHOCOLATE PUDDING.

6 yolks,
6 tablespoonfuls sugar,
6 sticks grated chocolate,
6 whites of eggs, beaten,

2 oz. chopped almonds,
2 tablespoonfuls cracker dust,
1 teaspoon baking powder.

ALMOND PUDDING.

10 whole eggs,
1½ cup sugar,

½ lb. almonds, blanched and grated,
1 lemon, grated.

Bake in a medium oven; serve cold with wine sauce.

HOT PUDDINGS.

AUF-LAUF.

Line a pudding dish with any stale cake you may have, or with macaroons if preferred. Cover this with fruit and sugar, and put on the back of the stove to heat. Cover with sponge made of six yolks, six table-spoonsful sugar, six whites beaten to froth, and some chopped almonds. Bake quickly. Serve hot.

NOODLE PUDDING.

1 pint milk,	2 oz. butter, heated.

In this boil some fine noodles and cool, add five yolks, beaten, with five tablespoonfuls sugar, one pint sour cream, five whites of eggs, beaten stiff. Bake and serve with wine sauce.

STEAMED NOODLES.

Kuchen dough raised twice, rolled and cut into round pieces and raised once more. Then put them into a buttered iron pot with a cover, pour some stewed prunes over them and bake an hour. Serve at once.

DIMPES DAMPES.

One pint milk, flour to make a paste, salt, two table-spoonfuls brown sugar, one cup heated butter, chop-ped apples to cover it, then spread in buttered tins. Bake quickly.

APPLE PUDDING.

Two quarts tart apples, stewed and strained, sweet-ened to taste. Cool and add one tablespoonful lemon juice and four yolks, well beaten. Turn this into a buttered dish and bake half an hour in hot oven. Cool, then spread with the whites of egg beaten stiff, with four tablespoonfuls powdered sugar and one teaspoon lemon juice. Dust with sugar and return to the oven to brown. Serve either hot or cold.

KUGEL.

Soak five wheat rolls in water, then press the bread quite dry. Knead it with three-fourths pound raw suet, two heaping handfuls brown sugar, one tablespoonful molasses, cinnamon, cloves and lemon, one tablespoonful water, a pinch of salt. Mix very well together. Line an iron pot with alternate layers of above dough and stewed and stoned prunes. Bake two hours; baste often with prune juice.

MATZOS PUDDING.

3 matzos (soaked, pressed and stirred until smooth).	1 cup goose fat,
	¼ cup white wine,
	Grated rind of a lemon,
10 eggs beaten separately,	Sugar to sweeten,
2 large apples (peeled and grated),	½ teaspoon salt.

Stir one-half hour, and lastly fold in the beaten whites. Grease form well, bake in a moderate oven one-half hour and serve with wine sauce, six eggs, one cup weak wine, sugar to taste. Stir constantly until it thickens as it is apt to curdle.

PUDDING SAUCES.

VANILLA SAUCE No. 1.

1 tablespoon butter,
2 tablespoons flour,

2 cups boiling water,
¼ cup sugar,
1 teaspoon vanilla.

Melt the butter, add flour and stir until smooth; add the boiling water and sugar. Boil until thoroughly cooked. Add flavoring, strain and serve hot.

VANILLA SAUCE No. 2.

One-half pint milk, vanilla bean and sugar to taste, boiled together. Remove from fire. Beat two yolks, with a tablespoon flour, and then add the hot milk. Put back on stove and stir, but do not boil it. White of eggs beaten stiff, with a little sugar, and put on top.

SAUCE FOR ANY PUDDING.

One gill strawberry juice, one-half pint whipped cream, Maraschino and sugar to taste.

LEMON SAUCE.

2 cups boiling water,
1 cup sugar,
Grated rind and juice of
1 lemon,

3 heaping teaspoons cornstarch.

Mix the sugar and cornstarch thoroughly; add the boiling water. Cook eight or ten minutes, stirring often; add the lemon rind and juice, and serve at once. If the water boils away and the sauce becomes too thick, add more hot water until the right consistency.

KIRSCH SAUCE.

1 pt. cold water,   ½ pt. granulated sugar.

Place on hot fire. Mix one ounce cornstarch in one gill of cold water, and when the water in sauce pan is boiling, add cornstarch and stir for two minutes. Remove from fire and add one-half gill Kirsch and stir again. Strain and serve with pudding.

WINE SAUCE FOR PUDDING.

Beat into the yolks of three eggs enough pulverized sugar to thicken them, add one-half wineglass of brandy and stir in the whites of the eggs, beaten to a stiff froth the last thing.

HARD SAUCE.

⅓ cup butter,
⅓ cup powdered sugar,

⅛ teaspoon lemon extract,
⅔ teaspoon vanilla.

Cream the butter, add sugar gradually, and flavoring.

CHAPTER XVI.

ICE CREAM AND FROZEN PUDDINGS.

GENERAL RULES.

Scald and then chill can, cover and dasher of freezer before using. Adjust can in tub, put in the mixture, then the dasher and cover; adjust the crank, and pack with finely chopped ice and rock salt; this must be higher around than the mixture is inside. Use three parts of ice to one part of rock salt for freezing, and use four parts ice to one part rock salt for packing afterwards. Ice cream must be frozen slowly and steadily; water ices steadily five minutes. Let stand five minutes, turn again five minutes; repeat until frozen. When mixture is frozen, remove ice and salt from top of can, wipe top and the cover; uncover and remove dasher, scrape it; beat the frozen mixture with a wooden spoon. Place heavy paper over it, put on cover and place a cork in the hole. Do not strain off the water until the mixture is frozen. Repack the freezer, putting ice on the top, cover with carpet or newspaper, and stand in cool place several hours.

A tightly covered tin can and a wooden pail may be substituted for an ice cream freezer, using a wooden spoon to scrape the mixture from sides and bottom of can as it freezes.

The ice must be finely crushed. Place in a burlap bag and give a few blows with the broad side of an ax or hatchet.

TO USE VANILLA BEAN FOR ICE CREAM.

Split a vanilla bean, or a portion of one, and heat it with the milk and sugar. Then remove it, and scrape out the seeds and soft part. Mix them with a little sugar and add them to the cream.

ICE CREAM FOR ONE.

One-half pound baking powder tin, a wooden spoon, a thick eight-inch bowl, or a small wooden tub, to form the outside of the freeze. Chop the ice fine. For each layer, use one-third cup rock salt and one cup of ice. The can must be water-tight.

½ cup cream,
¼ teaspoon vanilla,
4 teaspoons sugar.

Stir the ingredients until sugar is dissolved, and pack in can. Beat, and as it freezes, scrape from the sides of can with wooden spoon. Beat the mixture again, cover, turn the can back and forth until more of the cream is frozen. When frozen throughout, drain off water, beat the cream again, pack evenly, and put on cover. Repack in ice and salt to cover can, and let stand. Drain off water as it melts.

VANILLA ICE CREAM No. 1.

1 quart cream,
1 cup sugar,
1 cup milk,
1 teaspoon vanilla.

Scald the milk and dissolve the sugar in it; cool, add the cream and flavoring, and freeze.

VANILLA ICE CREAM No. 2.

1 pint milk,
2 tablespoonfuls cornstarch or flour,
1 cup sugar,
⅛ teaspoon salt,
1 egg,
2 teaspoons vanilla,
1 quart cream.

Mix flour, sugar, salt, and the milk gradually. Cook over hot water twenty minutes, stirring well; take from stove, add the well-beaten egg gradually. Cool. Add cream and flavoring. Strain and freeze. If cream can not be obtained, more eggs and flour should be used.

VANILLA ICE CREAM No. 3.

8 yolks,
1 cup sugar.
1 quart cream,
2 teaspoons vanilla.

Heat the cream, and pour over the beaten eggs and sugar and add flavoring.

CHOCOLATE ICE CREAM No. 1.

1½ oz. (squares) chocolate,	¼ cup hot water,
or ¼ cup prepared cocoa,	1 tablespoon vanilla,
1 cup sugar,	1 quart cream.

Melt the chocolate, add the sugar gradually, and then the hot water slowly. Cool, add cream and flavoring, and then freeze.

CHOCOLATE ICE CREAM No. 2.

6 yolks,	1 cup hot milk,
¾ cup sugar.	1 quart cream,
6 sticks Maillard's choco-	1 teaspoon vanilla.
late, melted,	

Stir egg and sugar, add grated chocolate, hot milk, cream and vanilla, and freeze.

CARAMEL ICE CREAM.

1 cup sugar,	1 scant cup sugar, melted
2 tablespoons cornstarch	to a brown liquid,
or flour,	½ teaspoon vanilla,
2 cups scalded milk,	1 quart cream.
1 egg,	

Make a custard of the first four ingredients, as in Vanilla Ice Cream No. 2. Then melt one scant cup of sugar in an iron spider, to a brown liquid, and add very gradually to the hot custard. Cool, add cream and flavoring, stir and freeze.

COFFEE ICE CREAM.

8 yolks, beaten.	1 cup ground coffee,
1 cup sugar.	1 qt. cream,
1 pint milk.	A little vanilla.

Heat the milk, pour over the sugar and beaten eggs and cook over hot water until it coats the spoon. Add cream, heat, and then the coffee grounds, cover tightly, and allow to infuse one-half hour. Strain carefully, cool, add vanilla and freeze.

CHESTNUT ICE CREAM.

3 cups chestnuts, cooked in milk,
A little vanilla,

3 cups sugar and 1¼ cups water, cooked to a syrup.

When boiling, add to six well beaten yolks. Stir until cold, and add one and one-half pints cream, one-half pound sugared fruit cut fine, and immersed in maraschino.

PEACH ICE CREAM.

6 yolks,
1¼ cup sugar.
1 cup hot milk,

6 yellow peaches,
1 quart cream,

Stir yolks and sugar together, add milk, grated peaches, and cream; freeze.

STRAWBERRY OR RASPBERRY ICE CREAM.

1 quart berries,
1 quart cream,
1 cup hot milk,

6 yolks,
2 cups sugar.

Press, strain fruit juice into beaten eggs and sugar, hot milk, and lastly add cream.

MAPLE ICE CREAM.

1 cup rich maple syrup,
1 pint cream,

4 yolks of egg,
1 white of egg.

Heat syrup to the boiling point and pour gradually on the well beaten yolk. Cook in double boiler until thick and when cool, add to the cream, whipped with the white of the egg; freeze.

CHOCOLATE SAUCE FOR VANILLA ICE CREAM No. 1.

1 oz. (square) chocolate,
⅓ cup cup water,

1 cup sugar,
1 tablespoon butter,
½ teaspoon vanilla.

Melt chocolate, add sugar, butter and water. Boil fifteen minutes, cool slightly, add vanilla, and serve with vanilla ice cream.

CHOCOLATE SAUCE FOR VANILLA ICE CREAM No. 2.

2 oz. chocolate,
¾ cup powdered sugar,

½ cup boiling water.

Stir and cook in double boiler to the consistency of molasses and serve hot with vanilla ice cream.

SHERBET.

In freezing sherbets or water ices, freeze steadily five minutes, let stand five minutes, turn again five minutes. Repeat until frozen.

FRUIT ICE.

1 quart water,
2 cups fruit juice or
crushed fruit,

2 cups sugar,
Lemon juice to taste.

Boil water and sugar to a syrup five minutes, cool, add fruit juice and lemon to taste; freeze.

NOTE—Orange, raspberry, strawberry, grape, currant, apricot, pineapple, etc., juice or fruit crushed, may be used alone, or in combination.

LEMON ICE No. 1.

1 quart water,

2 cups sugar,
¾ cup lemon juice.

Boil water and sugar to a syrup five minutes. Cool, add juice, and freeze.

LEMON ICE No. 2.

1 quart water.
1 pint sugar,

¾ cup lemon juice.

Make a syrup of sugar and water, boiled twenty minutes. Freeze and serve with crême de menthe.

LEMON MILK SHERBET.

1 quart milk,
2 cups sugar,

Juice of 3 lemons, or ⅛ cup lemon juice.

Mix in the order given, and freeze.

ORANGE FRAPPE.

1 quart water,
1 pint sugar,

1 pine orange juice.
2 lemons, juice only.

Make a syrup of water and sugar, boiling it twenty minutes. Add other ingredients, strain and freeze.

CREME DE MENTHE ICE.

4 cups water,
1 cup sugar,

⅛ cup creme de menthe,
Burnett's leaf green.

Make a syrup of sugar and water, boil twenty minutes and add crême de menthe and coloring.

CHAMPAGNE SHERBET.

1 quart water,
1 pint sugar,

½ pint orange juice,
½ pint champagne.

Boil water and sugar, cool, add other ingredients and freeze.

FROZEN PUDDINGS.

TO MOULD FROZEN MIXTURES.

Mixtures to be moulded must not be frozen hard, but should be solidly packed in the moulds and covered with buttered paper, butter side up. Fill moulds to overflowing. Repack in ice and salt, four parts ice to one part salt. Let stand several hours. At serving time remove mould, wipe carefully, and place in a vessel of cold water one minute. Remove cover, run knife around edges of cream, invert can on serving dish, and the frozen mixture will slip out. If necessary, wring cloth out of hot water and pass over the mould.

SIMPLE FROZEN PUDDING.

3 yolks,	4 oz. chopped hazelnuts,
3 tablespoons sugar,	Vanilla.
1 pint whipped cream,	

Mix in order given, and pack in a mould three hours.

STRAWBERRY PARFAIT.

1 quart cream,	½ pint strawberry juice.
1 cup sugar,	

Whip the cream, add sugar and fruit juice. Put into a mould and freeze three hours.

CAFE PARFAIT.

1 quart cream,	8 tablespoons Crosse & Blackwell's Mocha Essence,
2 whole eggs,	Sugar to taste.

Freeze quite soft shortly before serving, in glasses with whipped cream and maraschino cherries.

FROZEN NESSELRODE.

Boil one and one-half cupfuls sugar and three-fourths cupful water to a thick syrup. Stir till cool, and add four yolks. Put into a double boiler and heat this, cool again and add one and one-half cupfuls chestnuts which have been boiled and put through a ricer, one-fourth pound sugared fruit, one wineglass sherry, and one quart whipped cream. Pack tightly in mould and freeze four hours.

PINK AND YELLOW FROZEN PUDDING.

Stir five yolks with one-half cup sugar, flavor with two tablespoons maraschino, two sheets white isinglass (dissolved in as little hot water as possible), and half a cup hot cream. Mix the above together and put into a double boiler and stir till it is thick; cool and mix into it two-thirds quart whipped cream. Take the other one-third quart cream, put two sheets red isinglass (dissolved as above) into it, two tablespoons maraschino, mix well and line a melon form with it. Then into the center pour the yellow mixture. Close tight and pack in ice three hours. It fills a two-quart mould.

FROZEN COFFEE PUDDING.

6 yolks,
1¼ cups sugar stirred together,

1¼ cups cream,
1 cup hot milk.
1 cup strong coffee.

Cook all in a double boiler till thick, then break into this four sheets isinglass. When real thick, remove from stove. Cool slightly, add six whites, well beaten, freeze in a form. Serve with whipped cream.

LALLA ROOKH CREAM.

5 yolks,
1 cup sugar,
1 cup cream,

2 tablespoons gelatine,
1 pint whipped cream,
1 small wineglass rum.

Make a boiled custard of yolks and sugar and one cup cream, add gelatine (dissolved in a little cold milk), remove from fire, cool, add rum, five whites of eggs beaten stiff, and whipped cream. Mix all well together and pack in a mould. Place the mould in ice and salt three hours. When serving, decorate with maraschino cherries, and some of the cherry juice.

FROZEN STRAWBERRY PUDDING.

Alternate well sugared strawberries and macaroons in a pudding dish. Then cook four yolks, one cup white wine until it thickens, pour it, when slightly cooled, over the strawberries and macaroons and pack in mould six hours. Serve with sweetened whipped cream.

FROZEN CHOCOLATE PUDDING.

3 yolks.
¼ lb. chocolate,
½ cup milk,

¼ cup sugar,
1 pint whipped cream,

Melt chocolate, sugar and milk, add yolks of three eggs, well beaten, and when cooled, add to the cream. Freeze three hours.

FROZEN MACAROON PUDDING.

1 pint whipped cream,
¼ lb. stale macaroons, rolled,

¼ lb. candied fruit, chopped,
Sugar to taste.

Flavor with vanilla or maraschino. Freeze three hours.

FROZEN KISS PUDDING.

1 quart whipped cream,
½ lb. ground kisses,

1 teaspoon vanilla.

Mix and put into a mould and pack in salt and chopped ice three or four hours.

FROZEN DIPLOMAT.

6 yolks,
1 cup sugar,
1 pint cream,
6 lady fingers,

Sherry wine to moisten the lady fingers,
2 tablespoons maraschino.
⅛ lb. candied cherries.

Separate the lady fingers and sprinkle with the sherry, cut the cherries in half, soak in maraschino. In a double boiler, scald one pint cream, add it to the beaten yolks and sugar. When thick, strain and cool. Flavor with vanilla, add one pint whipped cream, and freeze very firmly. Stand a mould in a pan of ice and fill with alternate layers of frozen cream and lady fingers and candied fruit. Have the last layer cream. Bury the mould, well closed, in salt and ice for three hours.

FROZEN EGG NOG.

1 qt. rich cream,
1 cup powdered sugar,

1 gill brandy,
½ gill rum.

Mix all and freeze.

CHAPTER XVII.

PASTRY-PIES.

GENERAL RULES.

Use pastry flour. Have all the materials cool as possible. Butter, or any other fat or drippings may be used. The fat should be cut into small pieces, not too fine, if a flaky crust is desired. Take one-half of the fat, mix with the flour, salt and water gradually, to a stiff dough, and then spread the remaining fat on the rolled dough. In mixing the dough, use a knife; roll the dough lightly in one direction only, and on one side with a little flour. Fold like a jelly roll, chill and roll thin to fit the plate, and bake it brown. Sprinkle bread crumbs on lower crust before filling, to absorb extra moisture. If upper crust is used, slash or prick with fork to let the steam escape; moisten the edge of under crust with cold water and press the two crusts together at the edge. If under crust is desired very crisp, lay in plate and prick all over sides and bottom with a fork to help to keep its shape; bake well in hot oven. Fill the baked crust with the desired mixture. If filling should be set or browned, return to oven a few moments.

PLAIN PIE CRUST No. 1.

1¼ cup flour,   1 teaspoon salt,
¼ cup butter or other fat,   Cold water to mix to a
                             dough.

Mix one-half the butter with the flour, add water and salt gradually. Roll and spread the remaining butter on the dough. Fold as you would a napkin and roll to use.

PLAIN PIE CRUST No. 2.
(Cooky Dough.)

2 tablespoons butter,
½ cup milk,
½ cup sugar,
1 egg,

2 cups flour,
1 teaspoon baking powder.

Mix dry ingredients. Add slightly beaten eggs to milk and combine the two mixtures. Roll one-fourth inch thick. This makes dough enough for two oblong flat pans.

NOTE—Nice for apple, cheese, blueberry, or any other fresh fruit pie.

RICH PIE CRUST.

1 lb. flour,
1 lb. butter,
1 tablespoon vinegar,

½ rind of lemon,
A little salt,
A little sugar,
A little cold water.

Cut the butter in the flour and add other ingredients.

MURBERTEIG No. 1.

Five hard-boiled yolks of eggs rubbed to a paste, and one whole raw egg added.

½ lb. sugar,
¾ lb. butter,
¾ lb. flour,

¾ lemon (juice),
A little mace.

Mix all ingredients and press dough into pie plates very thin with fingers, since it will be impossible to roll it.

MURBERTEIG No. 2.

One-fourth pound butter and one-half cup sugar, stirred to a cream; yolks of two eggs, teaspoon brandy, rind of one lemon, and some of the juice; flour enough to roll.

APPLE PIE.

4 apples, medium size,
Flavor with cinnamon, nutmeg or lemon juice.

½ cup sugar,
1 or 2 tablespoons water, if apples are not juicy.

Pare, core and slice the apples. Line a pie plate with plain pie crust. Lay in the apples, sprinkle with sugar and spices if wanted. Cover with upper crust and bake until the crust is brown and the fruit is soft.

LEMON PIE No. 1.

¼ cup flour or cornstarch,	2 eggs,
1 cup sugar,	1 tablespoon butter,
1 cup boiling water,	Juice and rind of a lemon.

Mix sugar and flour, add the boiling water slowly and boil until clear, stir frequently. Add the yolks of eggs beaten lightly and cook over hot water until the egg thickens; then add the butter and lemon. When the mixture is cool, place on a baked crust. (See directions in general rules.) The white of egg may be beaten stiff and stirred with the custard when taken from the stove, or it may be mixed with four tablespoons powdered sugar, spread on top and baked a delicate brown.

LEMON PIE No. 2.

1 large lemon, grated,	1 teaspoon cornstarch,
1 cup sugar,	1 tablespoon milk,
3 eggs,	½ teaspoon butter.

Beat yolks, add sugar, cornstarch, butter, lemon juice, rind and milk, and bake on a half baked crust. When cool, cover with a meringue, and bake light brown.

LEMON PIE No. 3.

Cover a baked crust with very thin slices of lemon, about one-fourth inch thickness of lemon. Cover this completely with light brown sugar and bake.

ORANGE PIE.

4 yolks,	Juice of 2 oranges and 1
1 cup sugar,	lemon.
1 glass of water,	

Bake crust first, and fill with above crème, after all the ingredients have been well stirred together. When partly cooled, add a meringue and bake again.

CUSTARD PIE.

One and one-half cups of scalded milk, two eggs, one-eighth teaspoon salt, speck of nutmeg. Beat the eggs. Add 3 tablespoons sugar, salt and nutmeg. Stir in the scalded milk. Line the plate with pastry, rolled thin, having it extend over the edge of the plate about one-fourth of an inch. Pinch this up around the edge, and pour in the custard. Bake in a moderate oven about thirty minutes.

PUMPKIN PIE No. 1.

To one cup of steamed and sifted pumpkin add one-fourth a cup of molasses, one-fourth a cup of sugar, one beaten egg, half a teaspoonful of salt, one-third a teaspoonful of ginger or cinnamon, and two-thirds a cup of rich creamy milk. Bake until firm in a tin lined with pastry.

PUMPKIN PIE No. 2.

1 cup, steamed and strained pumpkin,	⅛ teaspoon mace,
	Grated rind of ½ lemon,
¼ cup sugar,	½ teaspoon vanilla, if desired,
⅛ teaspoon salt,	
¼ teaspoon cinnamon, nutmeg, ginger,	1 egg,
	⅞ cup milk.

Mix dry ingredients, add pumpkin and lightly beaten egg in the milk. Bake until firm in a tin lined with pastry.

PRUNE PIE.

Press one-half pound of stewed prunes through a colander, to remove stones and skin. Simmer five minutes in their own juice, add sugar to sweeten, rind of half a lemon and cinnamon or spice to taste. Spread the mixture on a pie crust and bake well. Any other dried fruit may be prepared the same way.

MINCE MEAT FOR PIES.

8 lbs. lean beef, cooked,	1 quart boiled cider,
1½ lbs. suet,	½ lb. citron,
4 qts. green apples,	½ lb. sugared orange rind,
3 quinces,	2 cups molasses,
2 lbs. currants,	4 cups brown sugar.
2 lbs. raisins, seeded,	1 pint whiskey.

Chop or grind the meat, suet, apples, quinces and dried fruit and mix well with the other ingredients and season to taste with salt, pepper, allspice, cinnamon, and cloves. Cook slowly two or three hours and add one pint of whiskey. Keep until wanted in a cool place in Mason jars. Bake between crusts. The citron and orange rind may be omitted.

ALMOND TARTS.

8 yolks, beaten.	½ lb. shelled almonds,
¼ lb. sugar, stirred,	chopped.

Puff paste in tin tart-forms and filled with above. Bake eight minutes.

APPLE STRUDEL No. 1.

12 large sour aples,	¼ teaspoon salt,
1 cup stoned raisins,	1 cup warm water,
1 cup sugar,	1 egg,
½ teaspoon cinnamon,	½ cup butter, melted.
3 cups flour.	¼ lb. almonds, chopped and blanched.

Into a large mixing bowl, place the salt and flour. Beat the egg lightly and add it to the warm water, and combine the two mixtures. Mix the dough quickly with a knife; then knead it, place on board, stretching it up and down to make it elastic, until it leaves the board clean. Now toss it on a well floured board, cover with a hot bowl and keep in a warm place. Lay the dough in the center of a well floured tablecloth on table; roll out a little, brush well with some of the melted butter, and with hands under dough, palms down, pull and stretch the dough gently, until it is as large as the table and thin as paper. Spread the apples, cut fine, raisins, almonds if desired, sugar and cinnamon evenly over three-fourths of the dough, and drop over them a few tablespoons of melted butter. Trim edges. Roll the dough over apples on one side, and with the aid of cloth, finish ,rolling and trim edges again. Then twist the roll to fit the greased pan. Bake in a hot oven until brown and crisp and brush with melted butter. If juicy small fruits or berries are used sprinkle bread crumbs over the stretched dough, to absorb the juices.

APPLE STRUDEL No. 2.

Noodle dough rolled out as thin as paper. Spread it with plenty of butter, about one cupful, cover with chopped apples, sugar, lemon, raisin. Put plenty of everything into it, fold like a jelly roll and bake in well buttered pan about one and one-half hours. Baste with sugar water.

APPLE CHARLOTTE.

Line a pudding dish with short pie crust, fill with chopped apples, sugar almonds, one glass red wine, raisins, lemon juice and rind. Cover with pie crust and bake.

CHAPTER XVIII.

CAKES.
CUP CAKES AND SPONGE CAKES,

GENERAL RULES FOR CAKES.

The oven must be ready for baking, and the pans cleansed and greased before going to work. Use pastry flour. Sift once, then measure. Mix baking powder with flour and sift three or four times. Sift spices with the flour. Use powdered or finely granulated sugar. Fill corners and sides of pan that cakes may bake flat. Angel cake pans that allow the air to circulate under them when inverted and so arranged that the cake, when baked, may be cut out, require no greasing, remain moist and will not settle. Cakes are baked when the sides shrink from the pan. In baking a cake, divide the time into quarters. The first quarter, the mixture should begin to rise; the second quarter it should continue to rise and begin to brown; the third quarter it should continue browning; the fourth quarter, finish baking and shrink from pan. The heat must be moderate at first, that the cake may have a chance to rise before it browns over. The heat must be increased and the cake baked as fast as possible without burning. A pan of cold water placed in the grate above, if the fire is hot, helps to regulate the heat. Leave it in until the cake is nearly done. Layer cakes need more flour and require a hotter oven than loaf cakes. Cakes may be classed under two heads: Those that contain butter (cup and pound), and those without (sponge and tortes). Rub off cake with coarse grater, if baked too hard or burned.

RULES FOR BAKING CAKE WITH BUTTER.

Use a warm, not hot, earthenware dish and wooden spoon with slits to cream the butter. Add the sugar gradually, warm it slightly, and cream with butter. The whites and yolks of eggs should be beaten separately, and the yolks added to the sugar and butter, then add one tablespoon flour. Beat the yolks with a rotary (Dover) beater and the whites with a wire spoon, whip or fork. The bowl in which the yolks were beaten should be rinsed with the milk. The milk and flour are added alternately, then the flavoring, and the beaten whites. When fruit is used, save a little flour to cover it, and add before the whites. Butter cake should be beaten thoroughly.

CHEAP CAKE.

2 eggs,
1 cup sugar,
1 teaspoon butter,

1 teaspoon baking powder,
½ milk, scalded,
Flavor with lemon or vanilla extract.

Beat eggs very light with Dover beater, add the sugar sifted and stir well together. Mix flour and baking powder. Melt the butter in the scalded milk and mix alternately into the mixture with the flour. Flavor. Bake in a hot oven, in a shallow tin, until brown and well set.

PLAIN CAKE.

¼ cup butter,
1 cup sugar,
2 eggs,
1½ cups flour,

2 teaspoons baking powder,
1 teaspoon spice, or ½ teaspoon flavoring,
½ cup milk.

Mix and sift flour, baking powder and spices as directed. Cream butter and sugar, add the beaten yolks, then the flour and milk alternately, the flavoring and beaten whites last. Beat well and bake twenty to thirty minutes. Two ounces of melted chocolate may be used, added after the yolks of eggs, or two tablespoons of cocoa mixed with the flour. Raisins quartered and seeded, and sprinkled with flour, may be added just before baking.

LAYER CAKE.

¼ lb. butter,
½ lb. sugar,
5 eggs.
6 oz. flour,

2 oz. cornstarch,
1 teaspoon vanilla,
1 teaspoon baking powder.

Cream butter and sugar, add yolks; then cornstarch, baking powder and flour, vanilla, and lastly fold in the beaten whites.

WHITE CAKE.

½ cup butter,
1 cup sugar,
2 cups flour,
4 teaspoons baking powder,

½ cup milk,
½ teaspoon almond flavoring,
Whites of 4 eggs.

Mix and sift baking powder and flour. Cream the butter, add the sugar gradually. Add the flour and milk alternately, then the flavoring, and lastly cut in the whites of the eggs, beaten until stiff. Bake in a moderate oven.

GOLD CAKE No. 1.

⅛ cup butter,
¾ cup sugar,
1½ cups flour,
¼ teaspoon soda,
Yolks of 4 eggs,

½ teaspoon cream of tartar,
⅛ cup sweet milk,
½ teaspoon vanilla.

Mix and sift flour and soda. Cream the butter, add the sugar and beat thoroughly; beat yolk with Dover beater, when half beaten add cream of tartar and beat to a stiff froth; add this to the creamed butter and sugar and stir well. Then add milk and flour alternately and the flavoring, stir thoroughly. Place in prepared pan in a moderate oven, and bake from twenty to thirty minutes.

GOLD CAKE No. 2.

1½ cups sugar,
1 cup butter,
¾ cup milk,
Yolks of 12 eggs,

Rind and juice ½ lemon,
2¼ cups flour,
3 teaspoons baking powder.

Stir butter and sugar well, then add eggs, one at a time, stirring a half hour, add lemon and lastly milk and flour, alternately. Bake one hour in a moderate oven.

OLD ENGLISH FRUIT CAKE.

½ lb. butter,	1 teaspoon cinnamon,
4 eggs,	1 teaspoon cloves,
1 cup molasses,	1 teaspoon ginger,
1 lb. currants,	1 teaspoon baking powder.
1 lb. raisins,	1 glass brandy, or 1 glass
½ lb. citron,	grape juice.
¾ lb. brown sugar,	¼ lb. chopped almonds.
1 lb. flour,	Salt.

Sift together flour, salt, baking powder and spices. Cream butter and sugar, then add the eggs previously well beaten. Next the molasses and prepared fruit (the almonds and citron to be finely chopped). Lastly, stir in the flour and brandy or grape juice. Pour into pans lined with paper, and bake very slowly for three hours. These cakes improve by keeping, and should not be used for two months.

WHITE FRUIT CAKE.

Cream half a cup of butter. Add one cup of sugar, then half a pound blanched almonds, grated, three-fourths a pound fresh cocoanut, shredded. Beat the whites of five eggs until dry. Add a part to the cake mixture, then add half a teaspoonful of almond extract, one cup and three-fourths of flour sifted with one teaspoonful of baking powder, and the rest of the beaten whites of the eggs. Bake in a loaf. Cover with boiled frosting, flavored with lemon and mixed with grated cocoanut.

FRUIT OR WEDDING CAKE.

1 lb. sugar,	½ cup black molasses,
1 lb. butter,	1 tablespoon mace,
1 lb. flour,	1 teaspoon ground cloves,
12 eggs,	1 lb. almonds (blanched
1 teaspoon soda,	and chopped),
1 nutmeg (grated),	4 lbs. raisins (chopped and
½ lb. each of candied	seeded),
orange and lemon rind	4 lbs. currants (well
(cut fine),	washed and dry).
1 lb. citron (cut in long	
and short thin slices),	

Have fruits and nuts prepared beforehand. Line

the pans with three thicknesses of paper, butter the top
layer.

Cream the butter, add the sugar, then the eggs,
slightly beaten, and stir well.   Add molasses and
spices.   Mix nuts and fruits thoroughly, and sprinkle
half of the flour over them.   Add to cake mixture, and
lastly, add the soda sifted with the remaining flour.

Bake in a slow oven four hours, in deep large pans,
two-thirds full.

BLITZ KUCHEN.

½ lb. butter,	1 lb. flour,
¾ lb. sugar,	2 teaspoons baking pow-
7 eggs, beaten separately,	der,
	Grated rind of lemon.

Cream butter, add sugar and stir well; add the beaten
yolks, lemon rind, flour and baking powder mixed and
lastly fold in the beaten whites of eggs.   Blanch and
slice a few almonds and strew over the top with a
sprinkling of sugar and cinnamon.   Bake in a well
greased spring form in a moderate oven about forty
minutes.

DEVIL'S CAKE No. 1.

2 squares chocolate (2 oz.),	1 cup sour or butter milk,
3 tablespoons water,	1 teaspoon soda,
1¼ cups sugar,	Yolk of 1 egg,
½ cup butter (scant),	2 scant cups flour,

Heat and melt the chocolate, water, and sugar; when
dissolved, add the butter.   Set aside to cool.   Mix
buttermilk, soda and the beaten yolk, add the melted
chocolate mixture, and then the flour, and bake in two
layers in a moderate oven, reserving the white of egg
for the frosting.

DEVIL'S CAKE No. 2.

Part 1.	1 cup brown sugar,
1 cup chocolate,	½ cup milk.
Part 2.	
½ cup butter,	1½ cups sifted flour,
1 cup sugar (brown),	1 teaspoon baking soda,
3 yolks, beaten,	½ cup sweet milk,

Melt Part 1, but do not boil.   Cool it.

Mix Part 2—Cream butter and sugar, beaten

yolks, then Part 1; stir well and then add milk and
the flour mixed with the baking soda, and bake in
layers. Chocolate icing.

COFFEE CAKE.

1 cup butter,
2 cups powdered sugar,
4 yolks of eggs,
½ cup chopped almonds,
1 cup grated chocolate,

2 cups flour,
2 teaspoons baking pow-
der,
1 cup strong coffee,
4 whites of eggs to froth.

Cream the butter and sugar, add yolks, coffee, almonds, chocolate, flour and whites of eggs beaten to a
froth.

SAND TORTE.

6 eggs,
½ lb. sugar,
½ lb. butter,
¼ lb. cornstarch,

¼ lb. flour,
½ lemon (juice and rind),
1½ tablespoon rum.

Cream butter and sugar, add beaten yolks, mix flour,
and cornstarch and add to the mixture with the lemon
juice and rum. Bake in a round or square loaf.

MOLASSES CAKE.

1 cup sugar,
2 tablespoons butter.
2 eggs,
1 teaspoon cinnamon,

1 teaspoon soda, dissolved
with 1 cup sour milk,
1 cup N. O. molasses,
2½ cups flour,
1 teaspoon cloves.

Mix flour and spices.

Cream butter and sugar, add eggs and molasses and
the flour and milk alternately. Bake in a moderate
oven in two layers.

Frost with white boiled frosting to which one cup
of chopped raisins have been added.

ADA'S CARAMEL CAKE.

4 oz. butter,
1 cup sugar,
5 eggs,
½ cup milk,

1¾ cups pastry flour (sift
twice),
2 heaping teaspoons bak-
ing powder.

Cream the butter, add the sugar and stir well. Mix

baking powder and flour and add alternately the milk and flour and lastly fold in the whites beaten very stiff. Bake in two layers in a moderate oven.

ADA'S CARAMEL FROSTING.

¾ lb. maple sugar, scraped.	Butter, size of an egg,
¾ lb. brown sugar,	1½ cups cream.

Mix and boil slowly for forty minutes. Remove from stove and stir over ice until the proper consistency to spread. If too stiff, thin with cream. Dip knife in cream to spread.

SPONGE CAKES.

RULES FOR BAKING SPONGE CAKES.

For Angel, Sunshine, and other sponge cakes, where baking powder is used, sift once before measuring, mix with the baking powder and sift three or four times. Where soda and cream of tartar is used, mix the soda and flour same as the baking powder, and add the cream of tartar to whites of eggs when half beaten; beat yolks thoroughly until frothy, with a rotary beater and the whites with a wire spoon, until very, very stiff. Add the flavoring to the beaten whites; then fold the flour lightly through. Do not beat or stir after the flour is in, as this toughens the batter.

CHEAP SPONGE CAKE.

2 eggs,
1 cup sugar,
⅜ cup cold water,
1 teaspoon lemon juice,

1 cup flour,
1½ teaspoons baking powder,
¼ teaspoon salt,

Beat yolks thick, add one-half of the sugar, add the water and lemon juice, the remaining sugar, the beaten whites, and lastly the flour, mixed and sifted with salt and baking powder. Bake slowly in moderate oven twenty-five minutes.

SUNSHINE CAKE.

6 eggs,
A pinch of salt added to the eggs before beating,
⅓ teaspoon cream of tartar,

⅔ cup flour,
1 cup sugar,
Flavor with the grated rind of ½ lemon, or
1 teaspoon vanilla extract.

Sift, measure and set aside flour and sugar; then sift flour four times; separate the eggs; beat yolks to a very stiff froth; whip whites to foam, add cream of tartar, and whip until very stiff; add sugar to the yolks and beat; then add the beaten whites and flavoring, then fold in flour lightly. Put in moderate oven at once, in ungreased pan; will bake in thirty to forty-five minutes. Invert to cool.

SPONGE CAKE.

6 eggs,
1½ cup sugar,
1½ cup flour,

⅛ teaspoon cream of tar-
tar,
Pinch of salt,
Flavor to taste.

Make same as Sunshine cake; oven slow; will bake in twenty-five to forty-five minutes.

ANGEL FOOD.

Whites of 12 eggs,
1 teaspoon cream of tar-
tar,

1½ cups sugar,
1 teaspoon vanilla,
1 cup flour.

Sift flour once, add the cream of tartar; then sift four times. Then sift flour and sugar together four or more times. Beat whites very, very stiff, add flavoring and fold the two mixtures together very lightly and bake forty-five minutes in a moderate oven. Invert to cool; do not grease the tin.

POTATO FLOUR CAKE.

9 eggs,
1¾ cups sugar,

Scant cup of potato flour,
½ lemon (rind and juice).

Separate the whites and yolks of eggs. Beat the whites of seven eggs very stiff. To the well beaten yolks of nine eggs and the whites of two, add the sugar and lemon juice. Beat thoroughly, add the potato flour, and beat again. Now fold in the beaten whites very carefully, and bake slowly in a moderate oven. Bake forty to fifty minutes.

CHOCOLATE CAKE.

6 yolks,
1 cup sugar,
3 rolled zwieback,
1 teaspoon baking pow-
der,

¼ lb. chocolate, grated,
¼ lb. chopped almonds,
Lemon, cloves and cinna-
mon,
6 whites of eggs, beaten.

Stir sugar and yolks very light and add the other ingredients, lastly whites of eggs. Can be baked in a loaf or in layers with any kind of filling.

DELICATE ZWIEBACK.

6 yolks,
1 cup sugar,
1 teaspoon anise seed,
6 whites of eggs,

1 cup flour,
1 teaspoon baking powder.

Stir the yolks and sugar one-half hour, add flour, baking powder, anise and six whites of eggs, beaten to stiff froth. Bake in flat pan, one that is high on the sides so the cake can raise. When baked light brown, remove from pan and keep in a dry, cool place until the next day, then slice the cake and brown it on both sides. Dust with powdered sugar. This is very nice for invalids.

SEVEN LAYER CAKE.

5 eggs.
1 scant cup powdered sugar.

Beat yolks well and add three-fourths cup of sifted flour and the whites beaten stiff. Spread on seven tins (one-quarter inch high), well buttered and floured. When baked, remove from tins at once.

Filling: Three eggs, one and one-half cups sugar, three sticks Maillard's sweet chocolate and a little vanilla. Boil in double boiler, stirring constantly. When thick, set out to cool and then add one-half pound butter (scant); stir this well, spread between the layers, over top and sides. Let cool to harden.

ORANGE CAKE.

5 eggs, yolks,
2 cups pulverized sugar,
Juice of 1 orange,
Grated rind of orange,
½ cup water,

2 cups flour (sifted three times),
1 teaspoon baking powder,
Whites of 3 eggs.

Beat yolks light, add sugar, beat again. Then add water, orange juice and part of the rind and the flour and baking powder mixed. Lastly fold in the beaten whites of three eggs. Bake in layers in a moderate oven.

Icing. Whites of two eggs, beaten stiff, powdered sugar to spread and the rest of the grated rind of orange.

CHAPTER XIX.

TORTES.

RULES FOR BAKING TORTES.

Tortes are cakes rich in eggs and nuts; bread or cracker crumbs usually take the place of flour.

The nuts are chopped, rolled or ground fine, mixed with crumbs and spices. The eggs are beaten separately. Beat yolks with sugar and add nuts, crumbs and spices. Fold the whites in last. Bake slowly in moderate oven.

MOCHA TORTE.

6 eggs,	1 cup flour,
1 cup sugar,	1 teaspoon baking powder.
1 tablespoon Crosse & Blackwell's Mocha essence.	

Beat the whites stiff; add the sugar and into this, the beaten yolks; then the flour mixed with the baking powder and then the mocha essence. Bake in two layers in a moderate oven.

Filling No. 1: Serve with whipped cream, sweetened with powdered sugar, and three tablespoons mocha essence.

Icing No. 1: Confectioners' sugar, and water, stirred until smooth, and mocha essence to taste.

Filling No. 2: Two cups C brown sugar. Moisten with water, boil until it strings, and add one tablespoon butter and two tablespoons cream. Boil until butter dissolves, beat until thick, and cool; then add one tablespoon essence of coffee. Spread immediately between cake.

Icing No. 2: Beat the white of an egg, one cup of confectioners' sugar, one tablespoon cold water and flavor with mocha essence.

WALNUT OR ALMOND TORTE No. 1.

1 lb. English walnuts or almonds,	9 eggs,
1 cup sugar,	¼ cup grated chocolate,
	½ cup of fine cracker crumbs.

Chop the nuts, reserving twenty-three halves for decorating the top. Mix the chopped nuts and chocolate. Beat yolks thoroughly with Dover beater, add sugar, and beat again. Then mix with the nuts, crumbs and chocolate, and stir well. Beat whites of eggs with wire spoon and add lastly, just as in sponge cake. Bake in moderate oven forty-five minutes in prepared spring form.

WALNUT TORTE No. 2.

8 yolks of eggs,	8 grated coffee beans,
1 cup sugar.	8 whites of eggs, beaten,
½ lb. grated nutmeats,	Vanilla flavoring to suit
1 tablespoon grated bread-crumbs,	taste.

Beat sugar and yolks together and add the other ingredients; fold in the beaten whites last. Bake in two layers.

Filling: One cup chopped walnuts, yolks of two eggs, cooked in one cup of cream, sugar to taste, juice of a lemon. Chocolate icing on top.

WALNUT-DATE TORTE.

2 large eggs,	1 cup dates (cut fine),
1 cup powdered sugar,	2 tablespoons flour,
1 cup walnuts (chopped),	1 teaspoon baking powder.

Beat eggs very light, add sugar, nuts and dates and lastly the flour mixed with the baking powder. Bake in a slow oven one hour.

If desired for dessert, pour over a glass of wine and cover with whipped cream. The wine may be omitted.

DATE TORTE.

10 eggs,	1 teaspoon cinnamon,
1¾ cup sugar,	1 teaspoon allspice,
18 or 20 dates (sliced),	1¼ cups cracker crumbs,
5 tablespoons grated chocolate,	2 tablespoons wine, brandy or lemon juice.

Rub the dates to a smooth paste with the wine, brandy or lemon juice. Beat yolks, add sugar, beat again, add the dates, chocolate and spices and cracker crumbs and stir in well, and lastly fold in the beaten whites of the eggs. Bake in a good sized spring form forty minutes.

NOTE—Prunes may be used instead of dates.

KISS TORTE.

6 whites of eggs,	1 teaspoon vanilla,
2 cups granulated sugar,	1 teaspoon vinegar.

Beat the whites of six fresh eggs to a stiff dry froth, add the sugar a little at a time and beat, add the vanilla and vinegar. Bake in a slow oven in two pans.

Grease a spring form and pour in it two-thirds of the mixture. Make small kisses dropped from a teaspoon with the rest of the mixture and form in a circle the same size of the spring form. Bake forty-five to sixty minutes in slow oven. Fill with whipped cream and berries.

ALMOND TORTE.

9 eggs,	4 stale lady fingers,
9 tablespoons granulated sugar,	1 teaspoon baking powder,
¼ lb. sweet almonds,	½ teaspoon vanilla.
⅛ lb. bitter almonds,	

Beat the yolks and sugar until very light; add grated almonds, grated lady fingers, vanilla, and the baking powder, lastly the whites of the eggs, beaten to a stiff froth. Place in spring form and bake in moderate oven about forty minutes.

DAISY TORTE.

10 yolks of eggs,
1 cup sugar,
¾ cup sweet chocolate,
¾ cup sweet almonds,
8 bitter almonds,
1 cup stale wheat bread crumbs,

½ teaspoon cinnamon,
⅛ teaspoon cloves,
1 teaspoon baking powder.
1 lemon, juice and rind,
1 teaspoon brandy,
10 whites of eggs, beaten,

Stir yolks and sugar together. Mix dry ingredients and add the rest, beaten whites lastly. Bake in three layers in moderate oven.

Filling: Two teaspoons of cornstarch, one cup of milk, one-fourth cup of sugar, two yolks of eggs, and flavor with vanilla. Cook all in a double boiler until thick. Cover the top layer with a chocolate icing.

POTATO CHOCOLATE TORTE.

1 cup of butter,
2 cups of sugar,
½ cup of cream,
1 cup potatoes, boiled and riced,
1 cup of almonds, grated,
1 cup of chocolate, grated,

4 yolks of eggs.
1½ cups of sifted flour,
1 teaspoon vanilla,
Rind of lemon,
2 teaspoons baking powder,
Beat 4 whites of egg.

Cream the butter and sugar together, add one yolk of egg at a time, and the rest of the above ingredients, beaten whites lastly. Bake in spring form, moderate oven, forty-five minutes. Chocolate icing on top.

HIMMEL TORTE.

¾ lb. butter,
4 tablespoons sugar,
4 yolks of eggs,

1 lb. flour,
1 rind of lemon, grated.

Cream the butter and sugar together and add yolks of eggs, one at a time; then the flour and grated lemon rind. Bake in three layers. Spread the top of each layer with white of egg to moisten, a sprinkling of cinnamon, sugar and chopped almonds. Put raspberry jelly on top of two layers, and the following crême over all: One pint thick sour cream, vanilla, two tablespoons cornstarch and sugar mixed. Boil and lastly stir in the beaten yolks of two eggs.

RYE BREAD TORTE.

10 yolks of eggs.	A little citron, chopped,
2 cups of sugar,	3 tablespoons preserved
1¾ cups rye bread crumbs,	fruit, or stewed,
1 cup grated chocolate,	1 wineglass claret,
½ teaspoon cinnamon,	10 whites of egg, beaten,
¼ teaspoon cloves,	2 teaspoons baking pow-
¼ cup chopped almonds,	der.

Stir the yolks of eggs and sugar until very light. Mix the dry and then add the other ingredients, beaten whites lastly. Bake in spring form, one hour, moderate oven.

CHOCOLATE TORTE.

9 eggs (whites to snow),	½ lb. of Maillard's grated
1 lb. powdered sugar,	sweet chocolate,
sifted,	½ lb. grated almonds,
	1 teaspoon vanilla.

Beat yolks with sugar, add chocolate, almonds and vanilla, and lastly the beaten whites. Bake one hour, in spring form, moderate oven.

Icing: One-quarter pound Maillard's chocolate, one cup of sugar, one cup of milk; boil and add vanilla and yolk of one egg.

FILLED TORTE.

½ lb. flour,	1 yolk of egg,
5 oz. butter,	2 teaspoons brandy.
2 oz. sugar,	

Make a dough of above and roll out and spread in a spring form, cover with canned fruit (not too much juice), and bake. Then cover the top with a sponge made as follows:

6 yolks,	Rind of 1 lemon,
¼ lb. sugar,	Whites of 6 eggs, to stiff
¼ lb. grated almonds,	froth.

Stir yolks and sugar fifteen minutes, add almonds, lemon and whites, and bake a light brown.

FARINA TORTE.

6 yolks of eggs.	6 whites of eggs, beaten.
1 cup of sugar, stir 15 min-	1 cup farina,
utes, add	1 teaspoon baking pow-
1 cup sweet almonds,	der.
(grated),	

Mix in the order given, and bake in spring form, moderate oven, forty minutes.

HAZEL OR HICKORY NUT TORTE.

¼ cup finely chopped hazel or hickory nuts,
1 cup grated zwieback,
1 cup sugar,
½ teaspoon vanilla,
6 eggs.

Mix into nuts the crumbs. Beat yolks, add sugar, mix the two parts, and lastly fold in the beaten whites with the vanilla. Bake slowly.

HAZELNUT TORTE.

8 eggs,
8 tablespoons powdered sugar,
1 tablespoon flour,
1 teaspoon baking powder,
2 lbs. grated hazelnuts (leave some whole, for decoration).

Beat yolks and sugar very light, add grated nuts, flour and baking powder, lastly whites beaten very light. Bake in two layers. Have whipped cream between layers and on top of cake. (Fresh strawberries can be used instead of cream.)

ZWIEBACK TORTE.

6 ounces sugar,
6 yolks, beaten,
¼ lb. grated almonds,
Juice and rind of ½ lemon,
¼ lb. grated zwieback,
½ teaspoon cinnamon,
½ teaspoon cloves,
6 whites, to a froth,
2 teaspoons baking powder.

Stir sugar and yolks, mix dry and add the other ingredients, beaten whites last. Bake in moderate oven, spring form, and when nearly done, put a little wine and sugar over the top.

NUT TORTE.

Two cups sugar, yolks of five eggs beaten with the sugar, one-half cup chopped walnuts, one-half cup chopped filberts, three-quarters cup farina, one-half teaspoon baking powder, mixed with farina, and one-half cup zwieback, add the whites of the eggs (beaten light) last. Have tins well greased and bake in two layers. Serve with one quart whipped cream on top and between tne layers.

MOSS TORTE.

10 yolks of eggs,	A little citron, cut fine,
7 whites of eggs,	Rind of 1 lemon,
1 cup powdered sugar,	Juice of ½ lemon,
6 oz. almonds, grated,	1 teaspoon baking pow-
A little cinnamon,	der.

Stir yolks with sugar until light, add some of the grated almonds, lemon juice and rind; then citron, mixed with the rest of the grated almonds and lastly the beaten whites.

Bake in spring form or in layers and put whipped cream or a custard filling with grated almonds between. Slow oven.

LADY FINGER TORTE.

6 eggs,	1 cup grated almonds,
1 cup sugar,	1 teaspoon vanilla,
	6 double lady fingers.

Beat eggs thoroughly, add sugar gradually ·and stir well. Add to this the lady fingers, browned, grated and sifted, the almonds and vanilla.

Bake in two layers in a moderately slow oven.

FILLING.

3 yolks of eggs,	1 teaspoon cornstarch.
½ cup sugar,	1 cup chopped blanched
1 cup cream,	almonds.
	Vanilla.

Beat yolks, add sugar gradually, then add to the heated cream, cook until it thickens; moisten the cornstarch with a little milk and stir into the custard to make it more firm. When cool, flavor with vanilla and add the chopped nuts.

Icing: Spread top and sides with sweetened whipped cream flavored with maraschino and garnish with maraschino cherries.

POPPYSEED TORTE.

18 eggs,	Rind and juice of a lemon.
18 tablespoons sugar.	1½ teaspoons cinnamon.
18 tablespoons ground	1½ strips German choco-
poppyseed.	late,
¾ lb. grated almonds,	1½ teaspoons baking pow-
1 wine glass brandy,	der.

Mix poppyseed, almonds, cinnamon, chocolate and

baking powder. Beat yolks of eggs, add sugar and stir well, then brandy, lemon and the dry ingredients and lastly, fold in the whites beaten stiff.

Bake in large spring form in moderate oven. Grease the form.

MUSHKAZUNGE.

7 whites of eggs (un-beaten),	½ lb. granulated sugar,
½ lb. almonds, grated and unblanched,	½ teaspoon cinnamon,
	Rind of ½ lemon.

Mix and bake twenty minutes in a long pan in a moderate oven.

MARTZEPAN TORTE.

½ lb. flour,	2 tablespoons sugar,
2 tablespoons water,	2 yolks of eggs,
¼ lb. butter,	2 tablespoons water.

Mix flour, sugar and butter, add eggs and water, and roll out the dough.

Filling: One pound almonds, blanched and dried the day before, then grated. One pound powdered sugar, juice of two lemons. Place on fire until it cooks (or is very hot); take it off and stir a short time, add the whites of eight eggs beaten stiff. Line a spring form with the dough, put in the mixture, place strips of dough over the top and bake in a very slow oven one hour. Dust with powdered sugar and candied cherries to decorate.

CHEESE TORTE No. 1.

½ lb. cottage cheese (riced),	5 oz. almonds, blanched and grated,
6 yolks of eggs,	Rind of a lemon,
5 oz. butter,	1 teaspoon flour,
½ lb. sugar,	6 whites of eggs.

Cream the butter and sugar, add the beaten yolks and other ingredients, beaten whites last. Place in buttered spring form in moderate oven until well set, and when cool ice with chocolate frosting. If two layers are desired, double the recipe.

CHEESE TORTE No. 2.

¼ lb. sugar,	5 tablespoons grated
¼ lb. butter,	wheat bread,
¼ lb. cheese,	10 yolks of eggs,
¼ lb. blanched and grat-	10 whites of eggs,
ed almonds,	1 lemon.

Beat sugar and butter to a cream, add yolks, put cheese through a sieve, and add that and other ingredients and mix well and bake in buttered spring form in moderate oven until well set.

CHESTNUT TORTE.

1½ lbs. chestnuts, before	8 whites,
shelling,	2 oz. grated almonds,
8 yolks,	1 teaspoon grated bread
8 tablespoons sugar,	crumbs.

Boil chestnuts in a little milk and put through the ricer. Cream beaten yolks and sugar, add crumbs and nuts and lastly, the beaten whites, and add other ingredients. Bake in a spring form in a moderate oven until set.

CHAPTER XX.

CAKE FROSTINGS AND FILLINGS.

PLAIN FROSTING.

1 cup confectioners'
sugar,
2 tablespoons boiling
water or milk,

¼ teaspoon vanilla,
Or 1 teaspoon lemon
juice.

To the sugar add the liquid, a little at a time, until thin enough to spread. Flavor, stir and spread with broad-bladed knife.

ORANGE FROSTING.

1 cup confectioners'
sugar,
2 tablespoons orange
juice,

Grated rind of ½ an
orange.

Mix sugar and liquid, same as plain frosting, and add the grated rind.

LEMON ICING.

One-half raw white of egg, two ounces confectioners' sugar, and beat well. Add just one drop lemon juice. Beat again five minutes.

COLORED FROSTING.

1 cup confectioners' sugar,
1 oz. (square) melted chocolate, or

2 tablespoons fresh fruit
juice,
Or fruit syrup.

The strained juice of fruits, strawberries, cherries, grapes, etc., added to the sugar, a little at a time, until thin enough to spread.

BOILED FROSTING.

1 cup sugar,
⅓ cup boiling water,
White of 1 egg (beaten),

1 teaspoon vanilla,
¼ tablespoon lemon juice,
⅛ teaspoon cream of tartar.

Pour water on sugar and stir until dissolved. Heat slowly to boiling point without stirring, boil until syrup will thread when dropped from tip of spoon, add cream of tartar to the egg and then beat. Pour gradually on beaten white of egg. Beat with fork or heavy wire spoon until of the consistency to spread. Flavor. Spread evenly with back of spoon.

BROWN OR MAPLE SUGAR FROSTING.

½ lb. maple sugar, or	White of egg.
1 cup brown sugar,	⅛ teaspoon cream of
⅓ cup boiling water,	tartar.

Prepare same as boiled frosting. Brown frosting may be flavored with one-half teaspoon vanilla.

CHOCOLATE FROSTING.

To the boiled frosting add one ounce (square) chocolate, grated, and stir in syrup before adding the beaten white of egg.

SWEET CHOCOLATE FROSTING.

1 cup sugar,	½ cup milk,
1¾ bars German sweet	1 teaspoon butter.
chocolate,	

Boil until a soft ball is formed when dropped in cold water. Beat until cool enough to spread.

BOILED CHOCOLATE FROSTING No. 1.

2 oz. chocolate,	2 whites of eggs,
½ cup cream,	Vanilla,
	Powdered sugar.

Boil chocolate and cream and when cool add vanilla. Beat the whites to a stiff froth, add powdered sugar until stiff enough to cut. Combine the two mixtures, beat and spread.

BOILED CHOCOLATE FROSTING No. 2.

¾ cup sugar,	1 square chocolate,
Water to cover,	2 yolks.

Boil water and sugar to a thick syrup, add the grated chocolate and the beaten yolks. Thin with cream.

NUT FROSTING.

1½ cups sugar,	½ cup milk,
1 teaspoon butter,	¼ lb. chopped walnuts.

Boil the first three ingredients four minutes, beat until cool and add the chopped walnuts.

WHIPPED CREAM FILLING.

¾ cup thick cream,	White of 1 egg,
¼ cup powdered sugar,	½ teaspoon vanilla.

Set medium sized bowl in pan of crushed ice to which water has been added. Place cream in bowl and beat until stiff, with whip churn if possible. Whip up twice, that air bubbles may not be too large. Add sugar, white of egg beaten stiff, and vanilla. Keep cool.

WHIPPED CREAM FILLING WITH PINEAPPLE AND NUTS.

1 yolk,	½ cup whipped cream,
2 tablespoons powdered sugar,	1 cup nut kernels, or ½ cup nuts and ½ cup pineapple.

Whip cream, same as above, using one-half cupful nuts and one-half cupful pineapple, all chopped up.

CUSTARD FILLING FOR CAKES.

⅞ cup sugar,	2 eggs,
⅛ cup flour,	2 cups scalded milk,
⅛ teaspoon salt,	1 teaspoon vanilla.

Mix dry ingredients, add eggs slightly beaten, and pour on gradually the scalded milk. Cook fifteen minutes in double boiler. Stir constantly until thickened; cool and flavor.

Chocolate Filling same as custard filling, and add melted chocolate.

Coffee Filling same as custard filling, add one and one-half tablespoon coffee essence.

Orange, strawberry or lemon filling made like custard filling, adding the desired flavoring.

ALMOND-CUSTARD FILLING.

1 cup cream, heated,	2 teaspoons cornstarch,
3 yolks of eggs,	1 cup blanched chopped
3 tablespoons sugar,	almonds.

Beat yolks, add sugar and cornstarch. Stir the hot cream into this, boil until thick, stirring constantly and when cool add the almonds.

CHOCOLATE FILLING No. 1.

½ cup sugar,	½ cup grated chocolate,
½ cup milk,	Yolk of 1 egg.
½ teaspoon vanilla,	

Melt chocolate, add sugar and milk, and boil; when it forms a soft ball in cold water, remove from fire. Add beaten yolk and vanilla. Cool and spread between layers.

CHOCOLATE FILLING No. 2.

Beat two whites of eggs very stiff, add four table-spoons confectioners' sugar, and lastly, one-fourth pound Maillard's grated chocolate. Stir until smooth.

CHOCOLATE FILLING No. 3.

½ cup milk,	½ cup sugar,
¼ cup grated chocolate,	1 tablespoon cornstarch.

Mix dry ingredients, stir in the milk, cook until thick and when cool add vanilla to taste.

CARAMEL FILLING.

1½ cups brown sugar,	½ cup milk,
1 teaspoon butter,	1½ teaspoon vanilla.

Put butter in sauce pan, when melted, add sugar and milk. Stir until dissolved. Heat gradually to boiling point without stirring, thirteen minutes, or until it forms a soft ball in cold water. Remove from fire, stir until it thickens to spread. Add vanilla.

NUT OR FRUIT FILLING.

½ cup fruit (chopped fine),   Boiled frosting,
½ cup nuts (chopped fine).

To boiled frosting add one cup chopped walnuts, almonds, pecans, hickory, hazel nuts, chopped figs, dates, raisins, or selected prunes, separately or in combination.

WALNUT FILLING.

½ lb. grated walnuts,   ½ cup granulated sugar,
¾ cup sweet milk,   2 yolks of eggs, beaten.

Mix eggs and sugar, add milk, then boil until it thickens, and then add one-half teaspoon vanilla, and the nuts.

CHAPTER XXI.

COOKIES AND KISSES.

PLAIN COOKIES.

½ cup butter,
1 cup sugar,
2 eggs,
½ cup milk,
2½ cups flour,

2 teaspoons baking powder,
¼ teaspoon vanilla or any other flavor.

Cream the butter and sugar. Beat the eggs and add to the milk. Sift flour and mix baking powder with one cup, then add the rest of the flour, and add gradually to make a dough stiff enough to handle. Roll on a floured board one-fourth inch thick. Shape with biscuit cutter. Sprinkle with sugar, cinnamon and chopped nuts, if desired. Bake in a quick oven ten to fifteen minutes.

WHITE COOKIES.

½ cup butter, or
⅓ cup beef drippings,
1 cup sugar,
1 tablespoon milk or water,

2 eggs,
1 heaping teaspoon baking powder,
Flour to roll out.

Cream the shortening, add the sugar, the liquid and eggs, beaten lightly, and the baking powder, mixed with two cups of flour, then enough more flour to roll out. Roll a little at a time. Cut out. Bake about ten minutes.

COCOANUT COOKIES.

Add grated cocoanut to white cooky recipe, and sprinkle a little on top.

JUMBLES.

Roll the white cooky mixture and cut with doughnut cutter, sprinkle with sugar and bake a delicate brown.

BUTTER COOKIES.

1 pound of butter,	2 tablespoons brandy,
1 cup sugar,	Flour to roll,
2 eggs,	1 teaspoon baking powder,
Rind of ½ lemon,	1 cup almonds, chopped
Juice of ½ lemon, or	fine.

Cream the butter, add the sugar, then the yolks of eggs, slightly beaten; add rind of lemon, and the flour mixed with the baking powder, then the brandy or lemon juice, with only enough flour to handle. Chill the dough, and when thoroughly cold, roll; cut with small biscuit cutter, brush with white of egg, sprinkle a little sugar on each cooky, and also some chopped almonds. Bake in hot oven a delicate brown. Will keep for weeks.

GOOD COOKIES.

½ lb. butter,	2 hard cooked yolks,
¼ lb. sugar,	mashed fine,
½ lb. flour,	1 tablespoon brandy,
2 raw yolks,	½ lemon (juice).

Stir butter and sugar, cooked eggs, add flour and raw eggs alternately. Roll thin, cut round and bake in greased tins. Chopped almonds, sugar and cinnamon on top.

FRUIT COOKIES No. 1.

Add one-half cup stoned and chopped raisins to white cooky recipe, and roll about one-fourth inch thick. Cut in rounds and bake.

FRUIT COOKIES No. 2.

⅓ cup beef drippings, or	½ teaspoon soda,
⅔ cup of butter,	¼ teaspoon salt,
1 cup sugar,	1 teaspoon cinnamon,
2 eggs,	¼ teaspoon cloves,
½ cup molasses,	1 teaspoon nutmeg,
1 cup flour, and flour to	1 cup raisins,
roll,	⅛ cup of water.

Cream the shortening, add the sugar, the beaten egg and molasses. Sift dry ingredients with one cup flour and add to above mixture; add flour and water to roll out. Cut with cutter and bake in moderate oven. Stone raisins and chop or cut in quarters and add to mixture before rolling out. You can omit fruit and have spiced cookies.

CHOCOLATE COOKIES.

½ cup butter,
1 cup sugar,
1 egg,
¼ teaspoon salt,
2 squares (2 oz.) chocolate,

2½ cups flour (scant),
2 teaspoons baking powder,
¼ cup milk.

Cream the butter, add sugar gradually, egg well beaten, salt and chocolate (melted). Beat well and add flour, mixed and sifted with baking powder alternately with milk. Chill, roll very thin, then shape with a small cutter, first dipped in flour, and bake in a hot oven.

PEANUT COOKIES.

2 tablespoons butter,
¼ cup sugar,
1 egg,
½ cup flour,
1 teaspoon baking powder,

¼ teaspoon salt,
2 tablespoons milk,
½ cup finely rolled peanuts,
½ teaspoon lemon juice.

Cream the butter, add sugar and egg, well beaten. Sift and mix flour, salt and baking powder, and add to first mixture; then add milk, peanuts and lemon juice. Drop from a teaspoon on an unbuttered sheet one inch apart. Bake in moderate oven twelve to fifteen minutes. Makes twenty-four cookies.

SPICED COOKIES No. 1.

5 whole eggs,
1 lb. brown sugar,
2 teaspoons cinnamon,
1 teaspoon ground cloves,

1 teaspoon vanilla,
1 teaspoon ginger,
1 teaspoon baking soda,
Flour to roll.

Mix the above together, add enough flour to handle it, roll into small balls and bake on greased pans.

SPICED COOKIES No. 2.

½ cup butter,
2 cups brown sugar,
4 eggs,
1 teaspoon each of cloves and cinnamon,

4 cups flour,
2 teaspoons baking powder.

Cream butter and sugar, add the eggs beaten slightly one at a time, then the flour. Roll out and bake as the above cookies.

MOLASSES COOKIES No. 1.

1¼ to 1½ cups flour,
½ tablespoon ginger,
½ teaspoon soda,
¼ cup fat or drippings,

½ teaspoon salt,
½ cup molasses,
1 tablespoon warm
water.

Sift dry ingredients. Mix the remaining ones, and combine the two mixtures. Roll, cut and bake as other cookies in hot oven, ten minutes.

MOLASSES COOKIES No. 2.

½ lb. butter,
1 pint molasses,
1 cup brown suagr,

2 whole eggs,
1 teaspoon baking soda.

Boil the butter and molasses together. Cool slightly and add two whole eggs, cinnamon, cloves and ginger to taste, brown sugar, flour to thicken, and one teaspoon baking soda. Roll out thin, cut round and bake on greased pans.

ANISE COOKIES No. 1.

7 whole eggs,
1 lb. powdered sugar,

1 lb. flour,
Anise to taste.

Stand the dish in hot water while stirring the eggs and sugar together; add the flour, which has been slightly dried, anise seed last, and bake on floured tins.

ANISE COOKIES No. 2.

6 eggs,   1 lb. granulated sugar,

Stir three-fourths hour, add one pound flour and stir one-fourth hour. Then add three cents' worth of anise seeds. Drop on buttered tins with teaspoon. Then place in a cool place until next morning, and bake in slow oven.

CARDAMOM COOKIES.

9 oz. butter,
9 oz. sugar,
2 whole eggs,

15 oz. flour,
1 oz. cardamom seed,
crushed,
Rind of 1 lemon.

Stir butter and sugar together, and add the other ingredients. Roll, cut and bake as other cookies.

CLOVE COOKIES.

1 lb. brown sugar,	1 tablespoon chocolate,
¼ lb. butter,	2 teaspoons baking
4 eggs,	powder,
½ oz. ground cloves,	1 lb. flour.
1 teaspoon cinnamon,	

Mix sugar and butter, add eggs, flour and the other ingredients. Roll, cut and bake fifteen minutes.

ROCKS.

1½ cups brown sugar,	½ lb. raisins (seeded and
1 scant cup butter,	chopped),
1 lb. walnuts (chopped),	2½ cups flour,
3 eggs,	1 teaspoon soda, dissolved
1 teaspoon cinnamon,	in ¼ cup hot water,
	A few grains of salt.

Cream the butter, add the sugar, then the eggs. Reserve part of the flour and mix with the fruit and nuts. Add the rest of the ingredients and lastly floured fruit. Drop from teaspoon on buttered tins, not near together.

LEBKUCHEN No. 1.

4 whole eggs,	1 teaspoon cinnamon,
1 lb. light brown sugar,	2 oz. citron, cut fine,
2 cups flour,	¼ lb. almonds, blanched
	and cut fine.

Beat eggs well with Dover beater, add sugar gradually, and beat again. Mix flour and cinnamon with chopped nuts and citron, and combine the two mixtures. Bake in three flat greased pans, in hot oven. When cool, cut into regular strips one-half inch wide, five inches long. Before taking out of pans, frost with one cup confectioners' sugar, two tablespoons water and flavoring to taste.

LEBKUCHEN No. 2.

Three cups brown sugar, one cup granulated sugar, seven yolks and three whites of eggs, to be well beaten together; half a pound blanched and chopped almonds, one-quarter pound chopped citron, one-quarter pound chopped orange peel, one whole grated lemon, two teaspoonfuls cinnamon, one teaspoonful cloves, six tablespoonsful wine, four whites of eggs, beaten very stiff, four teaspoonsful baking powder, five to six cups sifted flour. Mix well and bake in long pans, about half an inch thick, in moderate oven. While hot, ice with soft icing and cut into squares.

SPRINGERLIE.

Beat the yolks of four eggs until light-colored and thick, the whites until dry, then beat together. Add the grated rind of a lemon, and beat in very gradually one pound of sifted powdered sugar. Lastly add one pound of flour, sifted with one-fourth a teaspoonful of salt and a scant level teaspoonful of baking powder. Add the last of the flour cautiously, as all may not be required. Knead the dough, cover closely, and let chill two or three hours. Then roll, a small piece at a time, into a sheet one-eighth an inch thick. With a very fine sieve dust the sheet of dough lightly with flour, then press the wooden mould down very hard upon the dough, so as to leave a perfect impress of the objects on the mould upon the dough. Cut out the little squares with a knife and set aside, on a board lightly floured, over night. In the morning transfer to baking tins, buttered and sprinkled with anise seed, and bake in a slow oven to a light straw-color.

PFEFFERNUSSE.

Sift together two cups of sugar, four cups of flour, one tablespoonful of cinnamon, half a teaspoonful of cloves, one teaspoonful and a half of baking powder, and add half a cup of citron, grated or chopped fine, the grated yellow rind of a lemon, and a liberal grating of nutmeg. Mix to a dough with four large eggs, beaten slightly, without separating the whites and yolks. With buttered hands shape the mixture into small balls about the size of a hickory nut, and bake on buttered tins, an inch apart. The recipe makes about six dozen cakes, having the size and appearance of macaroons.

CHOCOLATE DROP CAKES.

2 whites of eggs,	1 teaspoon vanilla,
2 oz. grated chocolate,	1 cup powdered sugar,
1 teaspoon cinnamon,	1 cup bakers' bread
	(crumbled).

Beat the whites to a stiff froth, add sugar gradually, and continue beating. Mix chocolate, cinnamon and bread crumbs together. Add this mixture gradually to the eggs and sugar. Add vanilla and beat well. Drop from teaspoon on buttered paper or inverted buttered tin, not near together, as they spread. Bake in moderate oven twenty minutes, first ten minutes on floor of oven and last on rack.

CREAM PUFFS A LA DELMONICO.

¼ cup cold milk,	¼ lb. well-sifted flour,
2 oz. butter,	4 eggs.

Put into a double boiler, milk and butter; stir, and when boiling, immediately add flour. Stir briskly for two minutes. Then stand the dish on the table and add one egg. Mix briskly for two minutes, break in the second egg and mix again, and the same process with the third and fourth egg. Bake on floured tins, in a hot oven. Cool and cut them open on one side with a pair of scissors, and fill with the following boiled cream filling:

Filling: Place one pint of cold milk on the stove. Mix in another vessel two ounces powdered sugar, one ounce flour, one-half ounce cornstarch. Add two whole eggs and beat for two minutes. When the milk boils, add it to the other preparation. Stir one minute and put into another sauce pan and boil one minute. Add vanilla.

KISSES.

Whites of 4 eggs,	or 1 cup granulated
1¼ cups powdered sugar,	sugar.

The eggs must be strictly fresh and the sugar dry. Beat the whites until stiff, and gradually add two-thirds of the sugar. Continue beating until mixture will hold its shape. Fold in the remaining sugar. Drop mixture from tip of spoon in small piles one-half inch apart, on tins. Bake fifty minutes in slow oven or until dry. They are done when they leave the pan readily. Kisses require a decreasing heat.

KISSES WITH WHIPPED CREAM.

Prepare kisses same as in foregoing recipe. Bake thirty minutes on a wet board covered with letter paper, in slow oven. Remove soft part with spoon, and dry again in oven. When ready to serve, fill with whipped cream or ice cream, putting the kisses together in pairs.

NUT AND FRUIT KISSES.

To Kisses mixture, add chopped nut meats (almond, English walnut, hickorynut, shredded cocoanut), or fruit meats (chopped dates, raisins, or prunes), separately or in combination. Bake same as kisses.

COCOANUT KISSES.

Whites of 2 eggs,   ¼ lb. shredded cocoanut.
¼ lb. powdered sugar,

Make and bake same as kisses, folding the shredded cocoanut in last.

HICKORYNUT KISSES No. 1.

Whites of 2 eggs,   5 oz. hickorynuts.
5 oz. sugar,

Mix and bake same as kisses, folding the hickorynuts in lightly at the last.

HICKORYNUT KISSES No. 2.

2 yolks,   1 cup nutmeats,
1 cup sugar,   2 whites of eggs.

Stir yolks and sugar together, add nutmeats and the beaten whites of eggs. Bake same as kisses.

MACAROONS.

Four whites of eggs (beaten stiff). Add twelve ounces powdered sugar, and stir one hour; then add twelve ounces sweet almonds (blanched and cut with penknife). Drop on wafers. Bake in slow oven.

ALMOND KISSES.

½ lb. sugar, ½ lb. grated almonds,
6 whites of eggs, Vanilla.

Make and bake same as kisses, folding in almonds last.

CHOCOLATE MACAROONS No. 1.

¼ lb. sweet chocolate, 1 cup powdered sugar,
¼ lb. sweet almonds, Whites of 3 eggs,
  1 teaspoon vanilla.

Beat whites to a froth, then put in other ingredients. Drop with a spoon on tin. Bake ten minutes in a slow oven.

CHOCOLATE MACAROONS No. 2.

3 whites of eggs, ½ lb. grated chocolate,
¼ cup sugar, Vanilla.

Beat whites of eggs very stiff, add sugar, chocolate and vanilla. Bake on floured tins.

COCOA KISSES.

2 whites of eggs, ¼ teaspoon cinnamon,
1¼ cups sugar, Almonds, chopped and
2 tablespoons cocoa, blanched.

Make and bake same as Kisses, folding in the chopped nuts last.

DATE MACAROONS.

1 lb. dates, chopped fine, Whites of 4 eggs, well
1 lb. blanched almonds, beaten,
  chopped fine, 1 cup granulated sugar.

Add sugar to the beaten whites, gradually. Make and bake on greased papers in a moderate oven. One-fourth quantity of dates and almonds may be used.

CINNAMON STARS.

Whites of six eggs, beaten stiff; add one pound powdered sugar, and stir one-fourth hour. Then add three teaspoons of cinnamon, peel and juice of one lemon, and one pound grated almonds. Drop on buttered pan. Bake in slow oven.

ALMOND BOWS.

½ lb. almonds, shaved,   5 whites of eggs,
                         1 cup sugar and vanilla.

Stir in a double boiler until stiff. Bake on wafers.

PEANUT MACAROONS.

Beat the whites of three eggs until foamy. Add one-fourth a teaspoonful of cream of tartar, and beat until dry. Then beat in gradually half a cup of very fine granulated sugar. When all is in and the mixture is very light, fold in half a cup of sugar, one teaspoonful of flour, and one pint of peanuts, crushed or chopped to a fine powder. Drop by teaspoonfuls onto a tin lined with buttered paper, making smooth rounds. Sift granulated sugar on the top of each, and bake on the floor of a quick oven from five to seven minutes. English walnuts or other nuts may take the place of the peanuts. A cherry, or a bit of firm fruit jelly, or marmalade, pressed into the center of the top of each, gives flavor, when walnuts or pecan meats are used.

CHAPTER XXII.

CONFECTIONS.

GENERAL RULES.

Syrup boiled from sugar for candies must hang from the end of a spoon to form a thick drop, and long silk-like threads hang from it, when exposed to the air. The syrup is then 238 degrees Fahrenheit, and when a drop is tried in cold water, the water will remain clear and the syrup will form a soft ball and will just keep its shape. Boil a few moments longer, and try in cold water, and if the syrup becomes brittle, and it forms a hard ball, it is at 248 degrees Fahrenheit.

When the syrup begins to discolor it is at 310 degrees, while at 350 degrees it is caramel or burned sugar.. The syrup should only be stirred until the sugar is dissolved; if stirred while hot, it will grain.

PEANUT CANDY.

1 cup crushed peanuts,   1 cup sugar.

Shell peanuts and remove the skins. Take thick, unglazed brown wrapping paper, spread the peanuts over half of it, cover with the other half, and roll until well crushed with rolling pin. Warm sugar in oven, put into a frying pan and let melt to a syrup, stirring constantly until melted. Remove from stove, add the nut meats quickly, stir, and pour at once on a warm, buttered tin. Pat into a square with warm knives and cut into small squares immediately.

NOTE—Any kind of nut meats may be used.

MOLASSES CANDY.

1 cup molasses (New   1 tablespoon water,
    Orleans),   1 teaspoon butter,
½ cup sugar,   ¼ teaspoon soda.

Melt butter in an iron spider, add molasses, water and sugar, and stir until sugar is dissolved. Stir occasionally until nearly done, and then constantly. Boil until brittle or until it forms a hard ball in cold water. Set on back of stove, stir well, add the soda, stir thoroughly, and pour into a well greased pan. When cool enough to handle, pull until light colored and porous. Work candy with finger tips and thumbs, do not squeeze in the hands. When it begins to harden, stretch to the desired thickness, cut in small pieces with large shears, turning the candy half way round after each incision, thus alternating the direction of the cut. Cool on buttered plates.

VINEGAR TAFFY.

2 cups sugar,	½ cup vinegar,
	2 tablespoons butter.

Put butter into spider; when melted, add sugar and vinegar. Stir only until sugar is dissolved. Boil until, when tried in cold water, mixture will become brittle, or form a hard ball. Turn on buttered pan to cool. As edges cool, fold toward center; as soon as it can be handled, pull until white and glossy. Stretch and cut same as molasses candy. Any flavoring, vanilla orange, coffee or other extract may be had, by pour ing a few drops over the mixture, while cooling in pan.

DAISY CREAM CANDY.

8 lbs. sugar,	1 pt. water,
6 oz. butter,	½ tablespoon vanilla.

Mix in sugar and water, add butter and boil without stirring until it reaches 262 degrees Fahrenheit (see General Rules). Pour quickly on ice cold buttered slab. Flavor, when slightly cooled, and pull until white, glossy and porous. Mark into squares. Will be soft and creamy next day.

CREAM TAFFY.

2 cups sugar,	⅛ teaspoon gum Arabic
¼ cup water,	dissolved in a little
2 tablespoons vinegar,	water.

Stir all together until the sugar is dissolved. Boil without stirring until it will form a hard ball in cold

water and be brittle. Pour into buttered pan, and
when cool, flavor with vanilla or peppermint, and
pull until white. Cut into chunks.

FRENCH CREAM CANDY—STOCK DOUGH.

1½ lbs. XXXX confectioners' sugar,	¼ cup pure cold water,
White of 1 egg (strictly fresh),	Vanilla to taste.

Slip the white of egg in a cup; measure the space it
occupies; add the same amount of water (usually one-
fifth cup), and mix thoroughly. Pour enough XXXX
confectioners' sugar into the mixture to mould like
dough. Flavor to taste and knead thoroughly. This
forms the Stock Dough, and is the foundation of many
candies. Sprinkle board with confectioners' sugar, roll
one-fourth inch thick, cut into squares, strips, bars, or
any desired shape. It may be used with nuts, whole or
chopped, dried or candied fruits, etc. These candies
are better the day after they are made.

YELLOW STOCK DOUGH.

1 teaspoon yolk of egg,	XXXX confectioners'
1 teaspoon water,	sugar,
	Vanilla or orange extract.

Beat egg slightly, that it may be measured. Mould
with sugar, same as plain Stock Dough.

PINK OR RED.

1 teaspoon white of egg,	1 teaspoon raspberry juice
1 teaspoon strawberry,	or syrup,
juice or syrup, or	XXXX confectioners'
	sugar.

Beat white of egg slightly, that it may be measured, add fruit juice. Mould with the sugar as in
the plain Stock Dough. Needs no other flavor.

BROWN.

1 teaspoon white of egg,	1 teaspoon black coffee,
	Sugar to mould.

Measure egg, blend well with coffee, and mould with
confectioners' sugar, as in plain Stock Dough,
or melt chocolate with the plain Stock Dough.

WALNUT CREAMS.

Toss Stock Dough on bread board, sprinkled with confectioners' sugar. Roll with rolling pin one-half inch thick, cut into one inch squares and stick half a kernel of an English walnut on each square. Spread on oiled paper and let stand over night to harden.

CHOCOLATE CREAM DROPS.

Make cone shaped forms of the Stock Dough. Lay them on oiled paper to harden. Melt chocolate over boiling water, add a little cocoa butter; take the creams, one at a time, on a fork, or through a thin, long iron or fine wooden skewer, and dip into the melted chocolate to cover all sides. Set on buttered or waxed paper to harden.

MAPLE FONDANT.

Melt two pounds of maple sugar, grated or broken into bits, in a cup of boiling water. Boil without stirring to the soft-ball stage. Wash down the crystals that form on the sides of the pan with a brush dipped in hot water, and add, when about half cooked, one-fourth a teaspoonful of cream of tartar. Turn the mass on to an oiled marble slab or a platter, and let stand until a dent is left on the surface when the mass is pressed with the finger. Now work with a wooden spoon or paddle till the mass becomes a soft, smooth, creamy paste. Mould as you would bread dough a few seconds, then pack solidly in a glass or earthen jar. Cover closely with oiled paper, and let stand twenty-four hours or longer before using.

Cream or white fondant is made the same way, using granulated sugar.

FONDANT CANDIES.

Work a little of the fondant on a slab or plate, then form into balls, or thick lozenge shapes, with a candied cherry, or bit of fruit, an almond, pistachio, or other nut in the center. Let dry on paraffine paper, then dip into white fondant melted with a few drops of hot water over a sauce pan of hot water. Stir the fondant while melting and before dipping each piece of candy. Thin with hot water as needed.

COCOANUT BALLS.

1¼ cups sugar,	White of 1 egg,
⅛ cup boiling water,	Flavor with lemon extract.
¼ lb. shredded cocoanut,	

Boil water and sugar without stirring until it threads, pour onto well beaten white of egg, and continue beating until nearly stiff. Flavor, mix quickly with the cocoanut, and shape into balls.

CHOCOLATE FUDGES.

2 cups sugar, (maple,	1 teaspoon vanilla,
brown or white),	1 tablespoon butter,
⅔ cup milk or cream,	2 squares chocolate (2 oz.).

Melt chocolate over hot water or in oven, in a granite sauce pan. Add butter, sugar and milk gradually, and stir until sugar and chocolate are dissolved. Boil thirteen minutes, or until it forms a soft ball in cold water. Remove from fire to cool a little, then add vanilla and stir in one direction only until creamy, and the mixture begins to sugar slightly around the edge of sauce pan. Pour at once into a buttered pan, and when cool, cut into squares.

NOTE—If nuts are added, they should be chopped and mixed with the fudges before pouring into pan.

PEPPERMINT WAFERS.

1½ cups sugar,	6 drops oil of peppermint.
½ cup boiling water,	

Put sugar and water in granite saucepan and stir until sugar is dissolved. Boil until it threads or forms a soft ball in cold water. Remove from stove, add peppermint, beat until it thickens and looks cloudy. Drop from tip of spoon on slightly buttered paper.

Add a few drops of oil of wintergreen and color with fruit red for Wintergreen Wafers.

BUTTER SCOTCH.

2 cups brown sugar,	¼ cup butter,
	½ cup water.

Place in sauce pan over fire, and boil about twenty minutes or until a drop poured into cold water forms a hard ball. Stir constantly to prevent burning. Pour into buttered tins to cool. Cut into squares with heated chopping knife.

CHOCOLATE CARAMELS.

2 cups brown sugar,	¼ cup butter,
1 cup milk,	2 oz. chocolate.

Boil all together, stirring to prevent burning, until a drop will form a hard ball in cold water. Pour on buttered pan to cool and cut into squares with a heated chopping knife.

CARAMELS.

Put into a pan one pound of granulated sugar and a scant half-pint of cream. Mix it well, then place on the fire and let it boil ten minutes, stirring constantly. Now add a quarter of a pound of good butter. This should then boil to the hard ball stage. Remove from the fire and stir in a teaspoonful of vanilla. Pour on an oiled slab to the depth of about an inch, cut in squares when cool, then wrap in paraffine paper. Raspberry, strawberry, coffee or maple may be made by using these flavors and omitting the vanilla. For the latter use a cupful of maple sugar in place of the granulated sugar.

NEW ORLEANS PRALINES.

1 pt. pecan kernels,	1 cup cream,
1 cup brown sugar,	2 ounces butter,
½ cup New Orleans molasses,	½ teaspoon vanilla.

Boil sugar, molasses, cream and butter twenty minutes, stirring continually. Pour this over the nuts and stir until it begins to sugar. Spread on buttered plate.

ORANGE STICKS.

½ cup sugar,	Peel of an orange.
¼ cup hot water,	

Wipe the orange, remove the peel in quarters, and cut it in narrow strips. Place peels in sauce pan, cover with cold water, let boil up once and drain. Repeat five times, to extract the bitter taste. Heat the sugar with the hot water, and when dissolved, add the orange peel. Cook slowly until the syrup is nearly evaporated, drain and roll the strips in granulated sugar.

SPANISH PASTE.

¼ lb. raisins (seeded), ¾ cup English walnut
¼ lb. figs, meats,
¼ lb. dates (stoned), Powdered sugar.
¾ cup hickorynut meats,

Mix all together and grind fine or chop. Sprinkle board with powdered sugar, toss on the mixture, knead well, roll one-fourth inch thick and cut into small squares. Will keep indefinitely in a box packed in layers between paraffine papers.

GLACED NUTS OR FRUITS.

2 cups sugar, ⅛ teaspoon cream of tar-
1 cup boiling water, tar.

Put ingredients in a smooth sauce pan, stir until sugar is dissolved. Place over fire, see that the flame does not reach the sides of the pan. Heat to the boiling point, and let boil well, without stirring, until the syrup assumes a light color or just begins to discolor. With tips of fingers or brush, dipped in cold water, quickly brush off sugar if it adheres to sides of pan, being careful not to touch the syrup, as it is very hot. Remove sauce pan from fire and place in large pan of cold water, to instantly stop boiling, then quickly place in pan of hot water, to keep syrup from hardening. Now quickly dip fruits and nuts, a few at a time, in the hot syrup and remove them with fork or wire spoon to oiled paper.

Glacéd fruits keep but a day and should only be attempted in cold, clear weather. Oranges and tangerines are separated into sections and allowed to dry a few hours before dipping. Dip fruits first and then nuts, and do them quickly.

COMPOTE OF FRENCH CHESTNUTS.

Take fresh chestnuts. With a sharp-pointed knife slit each chestnut shell across one side. Cook a minute in boiling water, drain well, and let dry. Add a teaspoonful of butter for each pint of nuts, and stir and shake over the fire three or four minutes. Then remove the shell and skin together.

Keep the nuts covered with a thick cloth, as they shell better when hot. Soak the shelled nuts in cold water to cover, and juice of a lemon, seven or eight hours, to harden the nuts, drain and cover with plenty of boiling water. Let boil. Then simmer about two hours. When sufficiently tender, drain and cover with a syrup made of sugar and water, each equal in weight to the weight of the nuts, and a piece of a vanilla bean. Keep hot without boiling two hours. Drain off half the syrup, reduce about one-half, pour over the nuts, and keep hot one hour. Drain off all the syrup, strain, and reduce a little, and, when cold, pour over the nuts. If the syrup sugars when cold, add a little hot water, let boil, and use cold.

MARRONS GLACES.

Prepare the chestnuts as for the compote above. Dry the nuts, then take them one by one on a skewer, and dip into sugar and water that has been cooked until it begins to discolor. Follow directions for Glacé nuts or fruits. Lay the nuts on an oiled paper to cool. Remove the syrup from the fire as soon as the thermometer registers the proper number of degrees. If it becomes too cold, let stand in hot water.

CHOCOLATE SAUSAGE.

¼ lb. German sweet chocolate, grated,	White of ½ an egg, beaten slightly,
¼ lb. almonds (blanched and cut into chunks),	Sugar to roll.

Heat the mixing bowl slightly, add chocolate, almonds and the one-half of egg. Knead the mixture into a solid mass and place on board sprinkled with sugar and roll to resemble sausage. When ready to serve, cut in slices with a very thin sharp knife.

POP CORN BALLS.

Fresh corn does not pop well. Have fire hot; have enough corn in popper to cover bottom one kernel deep, and shake over fire; do not heat corn too quick. Continue shaking corn over fire after it has popped to "cook" it. Sprinkle with salt.

TO SUGAR POPPED CORN.

5 qts. of popped corn,	½ cup water,
2 cups sugar,	Flavor to taste.

Shake the popped corn, so that the unpopped kernels may go to the bottom of the dish. Put the nice white corn in a greased pan. Boil the sugar and water without stirring until it forms a soft ball in cold water or strings. Stir with wooden spoon into the popped corn. Mix and form into balls, lightly first with a spoon, and then with the hands (floured).

SALTED ALMONDS OR PEANUTS.

½ pound nuts,	1 teaspoon butter,
	Salt.

Pour boiling water over shelled almonds, allow them to stand until the skins will slip off easily. Drain at once and skin quickly. Place butter in a shallow pan, melt and add the nuts. Put on upper grate in moderate oven, and shake often, until slightly browned. Sprinkle lightly with salt, bake a few moments longer and take from oven, or fry the blanched nuts a light brown in hot fat and then salt.

CHAPTER XXIII

LUNCHEON AND PICNIC DAINTIES.

OYSTER COCKTAIL.

1 pint small oysters,	3 tablespons Rhine wine,
12 tablespoons Shrewsbury catsup,	Cayenne peper and salt to taste,
3 tablespoons tarragon vinegar,	Juice of 1 lemon.

Serve very cold with one-fourth teaspoonful grated horseradish on top of each portion.

SWEETBREAD COCKTAIL.

Soak a pair of sweetbreads in cold water one hour, drain and put into salted boiling water and cook slowly twenty to thirty minutes until tender; drain, plunge into cold water and when cold cut or break into pieces the size of small oysters. Put four or five pieces in each glass and cover with a highly seasoned lemon dressing and tomato catsup, one teaspoonful of each to a glass. Serve ice cold with a wafer.

Lemon Dressing. Juice of a lemon, equal quantity of water, salt and pepper to taste.

PATTIES.

Patty shells are made of very rich and light pastry in rounds with a cavity in the center. They are baked crisp. They may be filled with creamed oysters, chicken and sweetbreads, sweetbreads and peas, and chicken and mushrooms. They are served as a course for dinner or luncheon. The meat is cooked and cut in small pieces and heated in a thick, highly seasoned white sauce. Heat patty shells in oven; fill with hot mixture and serve. Rounds or squares of stale bread, cut very thick may be used in place of the patty shells. Scoop out the centers, leaving cases. Brush with melted butter and brown in the oven or fry in deep fat.

GOOSE LIVER PATTIES.

Place several small goose livers in milk and allow to remain one day. Drain. Some sliced truffles, salt and pepper. Smother in goose fat or butter, or both, until very tender. When cold, chop very fine; add the butter which they were cooked in, and a little Madeira wine; heat the mixture, fill into patties which have been heated and serve at once.

CUCUMBER JELLY No. 1.

Chop fresh pared cucumbers rather fine. To a cup add a cup of cool chicken or veal broth, three tablespoonfuls of tarragon vinegar, two tablespoonfuls of pickled nasturtium seeds chopped fine, and half an ounce of gelatine softened in one-fourth a cup of cold water. Season to taste with salt and pepper and set aside to chill. Serve cut in tiny cubes in tomato cups with mayonnaise or a boiled dressing, on lettuce leaves.

CUCUMBER JELLY No. 2.

Cook the cucumbers with a slice of onion until tender in boiling salted water, pass through a sieve, and season to taste. To each pint add half an ounce of gelatine softened in one-fourth a cup of cold water. Chill in a mould. Cut in cubes, and serve as before. As the water in which the cucumbers are cooked is use in the jelly, the quantity should not be large.

SANDWICHES.

Bread for sandwiches cuts better when a day old. Wrap in oiled paper to keep moist, or place in a tin box. Cream the butter before spreading. Any cold, cooked meat or nutmeats chopped fine and mixed with mayonnaise dressing is nice spread between bread for sandwiches. Nutmeats chopped fine and mixed with soft cream cheese, a little salt and cayenne pepper may also be used.

ANCHOVY BUTTER.

Cream one-fourth a pound (half a cup) of butter. Beat into this, very gradually, the sifted flesh of six anchovies, a tablespoonful of fine-chopped parsley, and two tablespoonfuls of chopped capers. To prepare the anchovies, drain from the oil, pick off the fins, separate the two fillets from the bones, and press the flesh through a fine sieve. If the anchovies were preserved in salt rather than oil, let stand some hours in milk or water to freshen.

ANCHOVY BUTTER ON TOAST.

Small, thin round pieces of toast, buttered; then spread very lightly with anchovy butter, and on this place a carefully fried egg. Garnish with lemon and parsley.

PEANUT PASTE FOR SANDWICHES.

No. 1. Crush the shelled peanuts, divested of skins, or pass them through a food-chopper. Season with salt and mix to a paste with cream, or omit the salt and add to creamed butter. Spread between slices of bread.

No. 2. Add one cup of boiling water to half a cup of crushed peanuts, or peanut meal. Dilute a teaspoonful of cornstarch with a little cold water and stir into the boiling mixture. Stir and simmer eight or ten minutes. Season to taste with salt, and spiced poultry seasoning. Spread between slices of bread.

CRAWFISH BUTTER.

Pick meat from the tails of twelve crawfish, dry the shells and pound them all together in a mortar, adding one ounce good butter. Place in a sauce pan on moderate fire, stirring until it clarifies (about five minutes). Strain through a napkin, letting drop into cold water. When it congeals, take it out, place in warm basin, stir until it assumes the desired color. Mix with the picked meat, season highly with salt and cayenne, and serve on toast.

PATE DE FOIE GRAS.

Take small goose livers, smother until soft in goose fat, mash into a paste, with three hard-boiled eggs, add salt, red pepper and a little grated onion, spread on small thin slices of toast.

SARDELLEN BUTTER.

Soak one-half pound sardellen, bone and mash them and add two tablespoons Neuchatel cheese, two tablespoons sweet butter, a little grated onion, a pinch cayenne pepper. Spread on thin slices of toast.

SWEETBREAD SANDWICHES.

Soak sweetbreads in cold water one hour, drain and cook in acidulated boiling salted water from twenty to thirty minutes or until tender. Drain, plunge in cold water and when cold chop fine. Mix with mayonnaise dressing and spread between bread for sandwiches.

BOSTON BROWN BREAD SANDWICHES.

Chopped walnut or peanut meats and dates mixed and spread between thin buttered slices of brown bread. Peanuts and figs with lemon juice instead is also a good combination.

STUFFED OLIVE SANDWICHES.

Chop stuffed olives fine in a wooden bowl, mix with a little mayonnaise dressing and spread between thin slices of wheat bread. Cut in triangles or circles.

LETTUCE SANDWICHES.

Wash and dry fresh crisp lettuce leaves, place between thin slices of buttered bread and spread a teaspoon of mayonnaise dressing on each leaf.

SARDINE SANDWICHES.

Skin, bone and mash sardines to a paste, add an equal amount of hard cooked eggs, rubbed through a sieve. Season with salt, pepper and a few drops of lemon juice, moisten with the olive oil. Spread between the slices of bread.

CHEESE.

COMPOSITION OF CHEESE.

Proteids, 31.23%.   Mineral matter, 4.81%.
Fat, 84.39%.   Water, 80.17%.

GENERAL RULES.

Cheese should not be tightly covered. When it becomes dry and hard, grate and keep covered until ready for use.

TOASTED CRACKERS AND CHEESE.

Prepare grated cheese, season with salt and cayenne pepper. Butter and cover each cracker with the mixture and return it to the oven. When the cheese is melted the crackers are ready for use.

COTTAGE CHEESE.

Heat sour milk slowly until the whey rises to the top; pour it off, put the curd in a bag, and let it dry for six hours without squeezing it. Pour it into a bowl, and break it fine with a wooden spoon. Season with salt. Mould into balls and keep in a cool place. It is best when fresh.

CHEESE SANDWICH FILLING.

Melt a tablespoonful of butter in a sauce-pan. Let this run over the bottom of the pan, then turn into the pan one-fourth a pound of cheese, cut fine or grated, and one-eighth teaspoon of cayenne pepper. Stir until melted, then beat in gradually the beaten yolk of an egg, diluted with one-fourth of a cup of cream and cook, stirring constantly until thick and smooth. When smooth, set aside to become cold in small jars.

CHEESE BALLS.

To one cup of mild creamery cheese add one-half cup fine grated bread crumbs, five drops of Worcestershire sauce and one egg well beaten; mix well and roll into small balls; place in wire basket, and just before serving fry in deep lard a delicate brown.

CHAPTER XXIV.

COOKING, PRESERVING AND CANNING FRUIT.

BAKED APPLES.

Wipe, peel (if desired), and core sour apples. Place in pan and fill the center of each apple with sugar. Measure one tablespoon of water for each apple and pour it around the apples. Bake in a hot oven until soft, but not broken, twenty to thirty minutes.

APPLE SAUCE.

6 or 8 tart apples,   1 cup water,
          1 cup sugar.

Pare, core and quarter the apples. Make a syrup of the sugar and water. When boiling, add the apples and cook a few at a time until tender, but not broken. Remove carefully. Boil down the syrup and pour over the apples.

RHUBARB SAUCE.

Skin and cut stalks of rhubarb in one-half inch pieces. Scald with boiling water. Let stand ten minutes and drain. Add water to keep from burning, cook until soft and sweeten.

STEWED PRUNES.

½ lb. prunes,   1 quart water,
        ¼ cup sugar.

Wash the prunes, and then soak them in cold water over night. Cook slowly in the water in which they were soaked until soft. Add one-fourth cup sugar to every two cups of prunes and cook five minutes longer. Season with lemon juice or cinnamon if desired.

TO PREPARE AN ORANGE.

Cut an orange in halves crosswise. Scoop out the juice and pulp with a spoon and place it on an attractive dish. Sweeten if necessary, or:

Insert a fork into the stem end of an orange; with a sharp knife, cut off each end of the orange, then cut the peel lengthwise through the skin to the pulp. Cut out each section separately, and put on a small plate in the form of a daisy. Put white sugar in center.

JELLY.

PREPARING THE JUICES.

Medium-sized granite preserving kettles are best to use in making jelly. They are lighter to handle and quickly and easily cleaned. Place the fruit in kettles, and to the small fruits add just enough water to keep from burning. Stand over a slow fire until they are thoroughly heated through and tender enough to crush readily. Stir occasionally, and when done pour into bags made of several thicknesses of cheesecloth, having them pointed so that the juice can run into a pitcher. Hang them up and let the juices drain out. For the first cooking do not squeeze the bag after juice stops running, as that will cloud it. When all has been drained the first time, squeeze the pulp well, so as not to waste any juice; this can be strained again, and if not so clear as the first, can be used for ordinary purposes. Do not make a large quantity at a time; a quart of juice is quite enough. Take equal measures of juice and sugar.

Put juice on to boil; let it cook rapidly for five minutes, then add an equal measure of heated sugar; boil a few minutes longer, or until, if a little is dropped on a cold saucer, it remains firm and round and does not spread. Skim and turn in glasses.

FILLING THE GLASSES.

First heat your glasses thoroughly, by standing in a pan of tepid water and allowing it to get scalding hot. Then set them on a damp cloth spread on the table or board. Pour jelly at once into these, filling almost to running over, as jelly will shrink. Let stand until cold. A thin scum forms at once on top of jelly, and this excludes the air. Cover, and keep in a cool, dry place. Melted paraffine poured on top of jelly makes a clean, air-tight covering.

CRANBERRY JELLY.

4 cups cranberries,   1 or 2 cups water,
                          1 cup sugar.

Pick over and wash the cranberries. Cook them (covered) in the water until they are soft and burst from the skins. Press through a strainer, add the sugar, and stir until the sugar is dissolved; stop stirring, and boil eight to ten minutes, or until a drop jells on a cold plate. Pour it into molds or glasses which have been wet with cold water and set away to cool.

CRABAPPLE JELLY.

¾ peck crabapples,   Water to cover,
¼ peck plums,   Sugar.

Wash and pick over the fruit. Boil the apples and plums in the water until the fruit is soft. Mash and drain through a coarse sieve. Do not squeeze. Place in bag and let drip. Take equal parts of juice and sugar. Follow directions for making jelly.

RASPBERRY AND CURRANT JELLY.

Take equal parts of raspberries and currants. Pick over the fruit, but do not take the stems from currants. Mash the fruit, using wooden potato masher. Cook slowly until currants are nearly white. Strain. Take equal parts of sugar and juice. Boil five minutes, add heated sugar and boil three minutes. Skim, and pour into glasses. Cover and keep cool and dry.

PRESERVES.

Fruit is preserved by cooking it with from three-fourths to its whole weight in sugar.

TOMATO PRESERVES.

1 lb. yellow pear tomatoes, or, the red ones, slices,	2 oz. Canton ginger, or a few pieces of ginger root,
1 lb. sugar,	1 lemon.

Scald the tomatoes to peel. Cover with the sugar, and let stand over night. Pour off syrup and boil until clear and quite thick. Skim, add tomatoes, ginger and the lemon sliced and seeded. Cook until the fruit is clear. Pour into jars or crocks.

GRAPE MARMALADE.

Pick over, wash, drain, and remove stems from grapes. Heat to boiling point and cook slowly until seeds are free. Rub through fine sieve. Return to kettle, and add equal measure of sugar; cook slowly thirty minutes, stirring occasionally to prevent burning. Put in jars or tumblers.

STRAWBERRY PRESERVES.

Select large sound strawberries. Pick and wash them carefullly. Place in preserving kettle alternately one quart of berries and one pound of sugar. Let stand over night. Place on stove, let cook steadily for several hours until the fruit is clear. Put in jelly glasses or jars.

QUINCE PRESERVES.

1 peck quinces,	¼ peck sweet apples (Tolman),
½ peck pears,	Sugar.

Wash and pick over the fruit, then peel and core. Cut the quinces and apples in rounds and the pears in quarters. Cover cores and peels with cold water, boil thoroughly and strain. For each pound of fruit allow three-fourths of a pound of sugar, add to the strained liquid and let boil until a clear syrup. Boil the rounds of quince in cold water until they can be pierced with a silver fork, remove carefully to platter and then into the boiling syrup. Add the rest of the fruit and boil slowly and steadily for three or four hours until the fruit is clear and a deep red color. Pour into crocks and cover.

ORANGE MARMALADE.

One dozen seedless oranges and four or five lemons Shave very thin, using all except the center pith and seeds. Then weigh the fruit, and to each pound add three pints of cold water. Set aside for twenty-four hours. Then put on fire, and boil gently until the rind is tender. Pour off, and set aside until next day. Weigh, and to each pound of material add one full pound of sugar. Cook until it thickens, about one hour, then pour into glasses. One dozen oranges make about sixteen pints of marmalade.

CANNING FRUIT.

GENERAL RULES.

Canning fruit is preserving sterilized fruit in sterilized, air-tight jars, sugar being added to give sweet-
ness. Fruits may be canned without sugar, if per-
fectly sterilized, that is, freed from all germ life.
Fruit should be fresh, firm and of good quality, and
not over ripe.

For canned fruit, allow one-fourth pound or more of
sugar to one of fruit, according to the acid in the fruit.
Boil the sugar to a syrup ten minutes, allowing about
one cup of sugar to two cups of water.

CANNED PINEAPPLES.

Slice and then peel and core the pineapples. Chop
rather fine, and to each quart of fruit allow one cup
of sugar and one cup of water. Mix fruit and sugar.
Let stand over night. Then add the cup of water
to each quart of the fruit. Pour in preserving
kettle, let come slowly to the boiling point, fill the
hot cans to overflowing with the boiling fruit, put
on clean rubbers and covers and seal at once.

TO BOIL FRUIT FOR CANNING.

Cook fruit until soft, only enough to fill one can
at a time, and remove, boiling hot, to the sterilized,
heated can. It saves time to have two or more
kettles of syrup on the stove, each with enough
syrup for one can. Add the fruit in rotation to the
boiling syrup, that one can may be taken up as soon
as the last one is done. Test if soft with a wooden
splinter or silver fork. When the can is filled with
the cooked fruit, pour over it to overflowing the
boiling fruit syrup; put on clean rubber, cover
and seal at once. The can must be air-tight. Wrap
the can in a cloth wrung out of hot water, or set in
a basin of hot water, while filling.

TO BOIL BERRIES FOR CANNING.

Pick over and clean the berries. If they require
washing, drain thoroughly. Allow one cup or more

of sugar to one quart of fruit, according to the acid in the fruit. Warm fruit and sugar gently until the juices flow, then simmer until thoroughly hot. Pour into hot jars and seal at once.

TO STEAM FRUIT FOR CANNING.

Wash, wipe and pare the fruit as usual and pack it carefully into the cans. Place the covers loosely over cans. Use new rubbers. Place the filled cans in crate of patent steamer or in ordinary kettle. Fill tank or kettle with cold water, to within an inch or two from top of fruit cans; place over a slow fire and gradually increase the heat to the boiling point. Boil berries slowly from 5 to 8 minutes, other fruit 10 to 30 minutes until sufficiently cooked; fill to overflowing with boiling syrup (2 cups water to 1 cup sugar—more or less sugar according to the acid in the fruit—and let boil ten minutes), seal quickly and set away to cool gradually. If ordinary kettle is used, place straw or thin slabs of wood underneath cans and wrap each can in cloth or straw, to prevent its breaking.

TABLE FOR CANNING FRUIT.

The sugar and water must be boiled to a syrup before adding to the fruit.

	For 1 qt. cans, Minutes.	Sugar, Ounces.
Boil cherries slowly	5	6
Boil raspberries slowly	6	4
Boil blackberries slowly	6	6
Boil plums slowly	10	8
Boil strawberries slowly	8	8
Boil huckleberries slowly	5	4
Boil small sour pears, whole	30	8
Boil Bartlett pears, in halves	20	6
Boil peaches, in halves	8	6
Boil pineapples, cut	15	6
Boil Siberian or crab apples, whole	25	8
Boil sour apples, cut in quarters	10	6
Boil ripe currants	6	8
Boil wild grapes	10	8
Boil tomatoes	20	8

CHAPTER XXV.

PICKLING.

Pickling is preserving in any salt or acid liquid.

PICKLED CHERRIES.

Pit the cherries and put into a large stone jar, cover with vinegar and leave it for twenty-four hours (stir it up a few times). Then drain off the vinegar. Measure the same amount of sugar as cherries, and alternate in layers, sugar on top. Stir this each day for three days, to dissolve all the sugar. Then bottle in Mason jars.

BRANDY PEACHES No. 1.

Boil peaches in thick syrup ten minutes and allow them to stand in that syrup over night. Drain and fill peaches in Mason jars. Boil syrup over again, until very thick, add brandy to taste, cool, and cover peaches with it and seal the bottles.

BRANDY PEACHES No. 2.

3 pecks choice peaches,   10 pints sugar,
                           1½ quarts brandy.

Peel the fruit, boil them until cooked through in a sugar syrup, and then put them on platters. Fill into bottles and cover with a new syrup made of the ten pints sugar boiled, and when taken from stove, the brandy added. Fill the bottles full.

PICKLED PEACHES.

Select large clingstone peaches. Pare, weigh and throw in cold water.

To seven pounds of peaches, add four pounds sugar, and heat slowly and boil about fifteen minutes. Add one pint of best pickling vinegar, small quantity of stick cinnamon, and cloves (soft heads removed), and

boil fifteen minutes longer. Now take up with a per-
forated skimmer, and lay them on flat dishes to cool.
Pack them in jars, let syrup boil until quite thick, and
pour over fruit scalding hot; when cool, seal.

SWEET PICKLED BEANS.

1 peck of string beans, cooked until tender,	1 lb. brown sugar, 1 tablespoon cloves,
1 quart vinegar,	1 stick cinnamon (broken).

Wash and pick over the beans, string and cut. Boil
in salt water (one teaspoon to one quart of boiling
water, until tender. Drain and spread out to dry;
then pack into air-tight cans. Tie spices in a bag,
and boil with the vinegar and sugar slowly, until a
nice syrup is obtained. Allow it to cool, pour over
the beans and seal.

RIPE CUCUMBER PICKLES.

Peel and slice one dozen ripe cucumbers, take out
the seeds with a spoon, sprinkle with salt and let stand
over night. Drain and boil until tender in one quart
of vinegar, one pint of water, one pound of sugar, two
tablespoons mustard seeds and one tablespoon each of
cloves and cinnamon tied in a bag. Place cooked
cucumbers in hot can, pour on the boiling syrup to
overflowing and seal at once.

SWEET SOUR PICKLES.

Five hundred tiny pickles. Salt pickles over night.
One gallon good vinegar, some stick cinnamon, whole
red peppers and sugar to sweeten. Let come to the
boiling point, throw in pickles and heat thoroughly over
slow fire. Bottle while hot, lay pieces of horseradish
and a few mustard seeds on each bottle and seal at
once.

GREEN TOMATO PICKLES.

1 peck green tomatoes (sliced),	¼ peck onions (sliced).

Salt and let stand over night. Drain well and cover
with good cider vinegar. Tie in a bag one ounce
cloves, one ounce allspice, some whole cinnamon and

one teaspoon Spanish red pepper. Add to the vinegar and tomatoes and cook one and a half hours. Then add one-fourth pound white mustard seed and two pounds of brown sugar. Let cook a while longer; bottle and seal.

CHILI SAUCE.

30 large tomatoes,
12 large onions,
5 large red peppers,

1 cup salt,
2½ cups brown sugar.

Scald, peel and chop tomatoes, onions and peppers; add all the rest, and boil two hours—until it thickens.

COLD CATSUP.

3 pts. of ripe tomatoes, peeled and chopped,
1 cup chopped celery,
4 tablespoons chopped red peppers,
4 tablespoons chopped onions,
4 tablespoons salt,

6 tablespoons mustard seed,
6 tablespoons sugar,
½ teaspoon cloves,
½ teaspoon cinnamon,
1 teaspoon grated nutmeg,
2 cups vinegar.

Mix and bottle; ready for use in one week.

TOMATO CATSUP.

½ bushel ripe tomatoes,
1 quart vinegar,
½ cup salt,
5 tablespoons mustard,
1 tablespoon cinnamon,

1 cup sugar,
2 teaspoons red pepper
1 tablespoon allspice,
1 tablespoon cloves,
1 medium sized onion.

Put tomatoes, wiped and quartered, on stove to boil, without water. When soft, strain through a coarse and then a fine sieve. Let stand over night, pour off the watery top and boil gently for two hours, with the onion, or small piece of garlic. Put in the rest of the spices, tied in a bag, and salt. Let come to a boil, and then add vinegar. Bottle and seal.

MIXED PICKLES.

100 small pickles,	1 horseradish root (diced),
1 qt. small white onions,	6 red peppers (small),
1 head of cauliflower,	½ cup mustard seeds,
1 pint of string beans,	¼ cup ground mustard,
1 carrot (diced),	Ginger root (a few pieces).
1 ear of sweet corn,	Hot vinegar to cover.

Freshen pickles by soaking in cold water a few hours. Soak cauliflower one-half hour, head down, in cold water, and separate the flowerets. Peel onions under cold water. Cut the corn, beans and carrot in small pieces crosswise. Mix first six ingredients well, salt generously, and pour boiling water over them to cover. Let stand over night. Next morning, drain and dry. Place in large vessel and mix thoroughly with the rest of the ingredients. Pack in crock, pouring the hot vinegar over them to cover. Lay cloth over top, cover with plate and stone, and keep cool and dry.

ESTREGAN PICKLES.

25 pickles (large, long ones),	2 tablespoons of whole white pepper,
1 stalk dried estregan,	12 laurel leaves (dried),
1 bunch of dill (6 stalks),	1 cup salt,
1 horseradish root (diced),	1 quart water,
	2 quarts vinegar,
	½ lb. mustard seed.

Soak pickles in cold water twelve hours, or over night. Drain and wipe. Place over each layer of pickles two or three blossom-ends of dill, three or four one-half inch pieces of estregan (stalks and leaves), a few small pieces of horseradish root, one tablespoon of whole white pepper, and three or four dried laurel leaves. Make a brine of two quarts of vinegar, one quart water and one cup of salt, beat together until it foams, and pour over the pickles to cover. Cover the whole with a bag, made to fit the top of crock. Fill bag with mustard seeds, and sew up. Cover with plate and stone, and keep in a cool, dry place. Must stand five or six weeks before they are done. Keep well.

SUMMER DILL PICKLES.

Pickles,	1 cup vinegar,
Dill,	Grape leaves,
Black peppercorns,	Salt.

Soak pickles in cold water over night, or twelve hours. Drain and dry. Place in layers of two rows pickles, then three or four blossom ends of dill and a teaspoon of whole black pepper; repeat, covering top layer well with dill and adding some cherry or vine leaves. To four quarts of water, take one cup of salt. Boil, and when cool, pour over the pickles to cover. Weight well with plate, to keep under brine. Let stand in warm place to ferment for a week. Then strain the brine, repack the pickles, put in fresh dill, and pour on the strained brine to cover. One cup of vinegar may now be added. Keep cool, in a dry place.

SMALL DILL PICKLES.

Select pickles of from two to three inches in length and scrub well with a small brush. Pack in layers in Mason jars, a layer of pickles, a layer of dill and a few mustard seeds, placing a bay leaf and a piece of alum the size of a pea on the top of each jar.

Let one cup of vinegar, two cups of water and one tablespoon of salt come to a boil. Pour boiling hot over the pickles and seal.

H. Jessen, CATERER.

181 MARTIN Street.   Telephone Main 490

FACILITIES FOR THE SERVICE OF BALLS, WEDDINGS, RECEPTIONS, PUBLIC and PRIVATE DINNERS, LUNCHES and GARDEN PARTIES, at Clubs, or at Residences, in every detail of the Catering Line, unequaled in the City.

FRAPPES and PATTY SHELLS a Specialty. Unequaled in the Northwest

The finest China, Tables, Chairs, Table Linen, Silver and Glasses to Rent.

——— PRICES REASONABLE. ———

ORDERS TAKEN FOR ANY PART OF
WISCONSIN,
ILLINOIS AND
MICHIGAN

Wares in the different Candy Shops may all look alike to you. Every dealer claims to make the purest and best.

My knowledge of making Candy covers a period of thirty-three years, and I claim that not one in a thousand uses the pure and best in the manufacture of what constitutes a Wholesome Confection. The unscrupulous merchant always sells at low prices, enabled to do so by the use of inferior grades of raw material and incompetent workmanship.

We aim to please and cultivate the taste regardless of price and strive for none better in America. We claim the distinction of being the oldest and only high-class Retail Candy Maker in MILWAUKEE.

GEO. TILLEMA.

Plankinton Hotel,   **MILWAUKEE.**

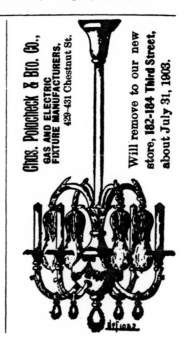